CHRIS BICKERTON

The European Union:
A Citizen's Guide

A PELICAN INTRODUCTION

PELICAN
an imprint of
PENGUIN BOOKS

PELICAN BOOKS

UK | USA | Canada | Ireland | Australia
India | New Zealand | South Africa

Penguin Books is part of the Penguin Random House
group of companies whose addresses can be found at
global.penguinrandomhouse.com.

Penguin
Random House
UK

First published 2016
001

Book design by Matthew Young
Set in 10/14.664 pt FreightText Pro
Typeset by Jouve (UK), Milton Keynes
Printed in Great Britain by Clays Ltd, St Ives plc

A CIP catalogue record for this book is
available from the British Library

ISBN: 978-0-141-98309-7

MIX
Paper from
responsible sources
FSC® C018179

Penguin Random House is committed to a
sustainable future for our business, our readers
and our planet. This book is made from Forest
Stewardship Council® certified paper.

www.greenpenguin.co.uk

Pour Mati

Contents

List of Tables and Maps

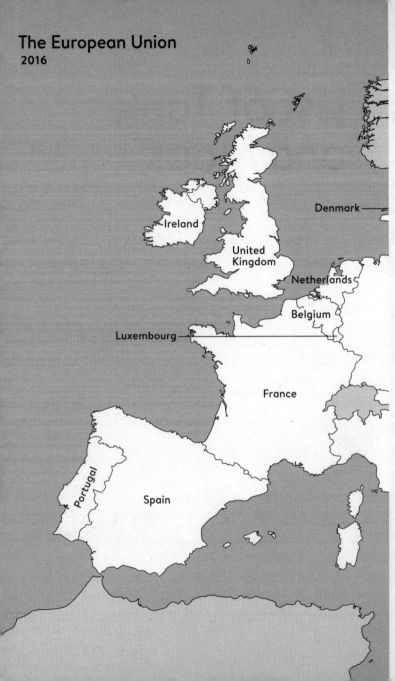

The European Union
2016

Denmark

Ireland

United
Kingdom

Netherlands

Belgium

Luxembourg

France

Portugal

Spain

PROLOGUE

Those who view the European Union as a super-state trampling on our national democratic freedoms exaggerate its power and authority. They ignore the small size of the EU administration and the central role played by our own national governments in the workings and decisions of the EU. Those who see in the EU an opportunity for creating a 'social Europe' forget the way the single market makes it far more difficult for national governments to curb the excesses of market capitalism. They also gloss over the fact that today's EU was built on the lost hopes of Europe's social democrats. Those who think the EU is a peace project, born out of the ashes of the Second World War, pay scant regard to the historical record. They attribute to 'ever closer union' achievements that belong elsewhere. Many people are convinced that for all of its problems and limitations, the EU nevertheless embodies our sense of belonging to something that we call 'Europe'. It is not perfect, they admit, but it is better than nothing. Its message is surely one of hope.

In this book, I have tried to describe the origins and workings of the European Union in a way that is as close to the truth as any account of this kind can be. Books can only be a perspective on a topic; they are never the final word. Some bits of the EU's story I have left out, others I have chosen to dwell on. But my goal has always been to describe the European Union as it is and not as we may wish it to be.

If we do that, then I believe we must ask ourselves whether the EU is the best that Europeans can aspire to. The EU appears to us as the only hope for our continent largely because of our pessimism about what we, as citizens, can achieve. My criticisms of the EU in this book do not come from a dislike of ambitious political projects. On the contrary, they come from a conviction that we can do better, that we can hope for more. The EU is fragile and survives because of our own lack of political imagination. Everything is up for grabs. It is time for Europeans to take charge of their own future.

ACKNOWLEDGEMENTS

For giving me the opportunity to write this book, I have to thank my editor at Penguin, Casiana Ionita. I am grateful for her confidence in me throughout the writing and editing process. My research for this book was mainly in the form of reading what others have written. I am grateful to all those who have gone before me and whose work I draw upon in the following pages. It goes without saying that relying on their work constitutes no endorsement whatsoever on their part for the arguments that follow.

A number of people read an earlier draft of this manuscript and provided me with extensive feedback, at very short notice. I am immensely grateful in particular to David Bickerton, Emilie Bickerton, Sarah Caro, Tania Oram, Peter Ramsay, Suke Wolton, Philip Cunliffe, Carlo Invernizzi Accetti and David Runciman. Their criticisms and suggested changes were of great help to me, as were their warm words of encouragement. All responsibility for the final product lies with me.

The Japanese novelist Haruki Murakami wrote a fun little book about the relationship between running and writing. His main recommendation to writers was to stay fit as writing a book is a bit like running a marathon. I swapped running for swimming but Murakami was spot on. My thanks go to the staff at Parkside Pools in Cambridge for keeping the swimming pool open and clean while I was writing this book. I would also like to thank the catering staff at Queens' College for providing hearty English stews and treacle puddings. I missed them greatly in those dog days between Christmas and New Year.

Writing a book is an act of selfishness measured by your ability to shut yourself off from others. Bridges will be burnt along the way. My long absences from my office in the department of politics and international studies were accepted with immensely good grace. I would like to thank very warmly my colleagues at the department, including Suzy Adcock and her superb admin team. Knowing that I was holed up in my college office trying to write this book, they left me very much alone.

But it is the people closest to you who bear the biggest brunt. This book would never have been possible without the complete and unwavering support of my wonderful wife, Ema. She suffered my writing absences and prodded me into action when my resolve began to falter. She put herself second in order that this book might see the light of day. She has taught me that there is no need to be 'in the zone' in order to write. Not even a decent cup of coffee or a clear head is needed. Just a laptop, snatched hours here and there, and someone who loves you enough to let you get on with it. The hardest moments were the many weekends spent working on the book and I am very sorry for those. I would have dedicated this book to her were there not another person in our lives now.

When I needed to take a break from writing, I would often look out of my window at Queens'. My office gives onto the river Cam and to the lawn in front of the Erasmus Building. During the week, I would see the children of the Queens' College nursery playing there, and sometimes I would see my daughter Matilda in her thick red winter puffer jacket. She would venture uncertainly across the lawn, pause for thought, and then be blown over by a gust of wind. But soon she would be off again, undeterred. Had I not had a book to write, I would have watched her all day. She has brought indescribable joy to my life and this book is dedicated to her with all my love and affection.

CHRONOLOGY

1952   The European Coal and Steel Community (ECSC) is founded by France, West Germany, Italy, Belgium, the Netherlands and Luxembourg

1954   A majority of French parliamentarians reject the European Defence Community

1957   The Treaty of Rome is signed, creating the European Economic Community (EEC) and the European Atomic Energy Community (Euratom)

1965   The 'empty chair crisis' when General de Gaulle removed the French representative from the Council of Ministers

1967   All three 'communities' (ECSC, EEC and Euratom) become known as the European Communities (EC)

1973   The United Kingdom, Ireland and Denmark join the EC

1975   The UK holds a referendum on its membership of the EC; a majority votes to remain

1981   Greece joins the EC

1985	The signing of the Schengen Agreement, which leads to the removal of internal borders within the EC
1986	The Single European Act is signed; Spain and Portugal join the EC in the same year
1992	The Maastricht Treaty is signed and the EC is formally renamed as the EU; the Danish reject it in a referendum
1993	The Danes vote in favour of the Maastricht Treaty in a second referendum
1995	Sweden, Austria and Finland join the EU
1997	The Amsterdam Treaty is signed by EU member states; it enters into force in 1999
1998	The European Central Bank is established
1999	The euro is created and national currencies are irrevocably fixed to it at an agreed rate
2002	Euro notes and coins are introduced into circulation; old national currencies are phased out
2003	A constitutional convention is established, tasked with drawing up a constitution for the EU. It is presided over by ex-French President Valéry Giscard d'Estaing
2004	Poland, Hungary, Slovakia, Slovenia, the Czech Republic, Cyprus, Malta, Estonia, Lithuania and Latvia all join the EU

2005   The French and the Dutch reject the Constitutional Treaty in referendums

2007   The Lisbon Treaty is signed; Romania and Bulgaria join the EU in the same year

2008   Ireland rejects the Lisbon Treaty in a referendum

2009   The Irish vote again and this time in favour of the Lisbon Treaty; the Lisbon Treaty enters into force two months later; the PASOK government in Greece announces that its budget deficit is much higher than previously thought – the Eurozone crisis begins

2010   Greece receives its first bail-out from the EU and the IMF; the Irish accept a bail-out deal with the EU and IMF

2011   Portugal receives an EU/IMF bail-out; the Schengen Agreement is suspended on the border between France and Italy

2013   Croatia joins the EU

2015   A migration crisis engulfs the EU, with around one million refugees arriving in Germany by the end of the year; some EU member states decide to close their borders to migrants

2016   The UK holds a referendum on EU membership; the Dutch hold a referendum on the EU's association agreement with Ukraine

Solving the EU Riddle

The European Union stands at the very centre of European politics. Terms such as the Eurozone, banking union, bailouts, refugee quotas and Schengen are regularly in the headlines of national newspapers across the continent. Some words, like Grexit and Brexit, have become part of everyday language. Conflicts involving the EU have a Hollywood blockbuster quality to them: during the 2015 Greek debt crisis, the steely German finance minister Wolfgang Schäuble was pitted against Yanis Varoufakis, the charismatic but controversial Greek finance minister. Some crises engulfing the EU have huge emotional resonance: few can be left indifferent by the footage of desperate refugees seeking to reach the shores of Europe, or by the stories of Greek and Italian pensioners killing themselves after having lost all their savings in the financial crisis. The EU is at the centre of these crises and solutions seem impossible without it.

And yet, in spite of this, the EU still appears as a monolithic and drab entity housed in buildings that somehow all look the same. It is a source of technical regulations, drafted by officials who rush from one meeting to another, far removed from the everyday concerns of European citizens. How many of us would disagree with Pope Francis, who warned the European Parliament in 2014 that 'the great ideas which once inspired Europe seem to have lost their attraction, only to be replaced by the bureaucratic technicalities of their institutions'? As a result of a bizarre sort of alchemy, conflicts loaded with moral and historical importance are transformed by the EU into technical discussions of detailed legal texts. Solutions invariably take on the appearance of a diplomatic fudge.

The EU has its supporters. They believe it stands for an incredible effort at overcoming the petty narrow-mindedness of the continent's nation-states.[1] It also has its critics, for whom the EU is a conspiracy whose origins lie in the boardrooms of multinational companies or in the archives of the German Third Reich.[2] But these two groups are in a minority. For most of us, the EU is unloved but unavoidable. We think of it with a sense of unhappy fatalism. Our temptation, however important the EU may be, is to turn away from it and ignore its intricate workings and dizzying acronyms.

A Citizen's Guide

Turning away from the EU may be a temptation, but it is a grave mistake. The European Union provides the mechanisms by which national governments across the continent rule. It is the sea in which national politicians swim. Contrary to what most of the EU's critics believe, from Nigel Farage and Marine Le Pen to Matteo Salvini and Geert Wilders, the European Union is not a super-state that lords it over its members. But nor is it, as its supporters would have us believe, a post-national federation that floats freely above the continent's nation-states, taming their violence and inciting them to be generous with one another. Governments have not given up their powers to Brussels; they are the ones that make the policies. But why does it not seem to operate in this way? Why does the EU appear like a stand-alone phenomenon, separate from its member states?

This is the great riddle of the European Union and one that this guide sets out to solve. The answer lies not with Brussels but with our own governments and our own societies. Over time, national governments have started to think of their existence and power as coming from their membership of the EU. In 2015, the Portuguese President, Aníbal Cavaco Silva, argued that EU and Eurozone membership were inscribed in the country's constitution and therefore outside the realm of party politics. In Greece, for all the anger directed at its European creditors and at Angela Merkel, there was no serious consideration of pursuing a life outside the Eurozone. Even in the United Kingdom, 'going it alone' doesn't seem to be an option. One of the most commonly heard arguments against Brexit is that if the UK leaves the EU, the UK as a union of four nations will break apart, with Scotland the first to go. In other words, a precarious and wobbly UK is being held together by the magical power of the EU. This view makes the UK rather like Bosnia-Herzegovina, a Balkan country on the borders of the EU whose complex and fissile political system survives only because of the prospect of EU membership. A YouGov poll found that many Brits don't believe that a vote to leave the EU in the referendum would lead to exit.[3] Most, including some of the leading figures of the Brexit movement, believe it should be used as a bargaining chip in continued negotiations with Brussels. Even for countries voting to leave, there is no easy way out.

This is the curious phenomenon of Europe's nation-states being transformed into member states, states whose very existence seems to depend upon their membership of the EU.[4] The power and strength that we attribute to the EU is really a reflection of the changing way in which governments across Europe legitimize their own authority. Rather than relying on the nation, as has been done since the nineteenth century, governments depend on their membership of the EU. Political legitimacy today comes less from the support of citizens and more from relationships forged between governments at the EU level. It is no surprise that exit from the EU appears so frightening to our political elites: it would deprive them of this crucial source of authority.

If we want to challenge this notion of political legitimacy and put citizens back at the centre of how a government exercises its authority, then we need to understand the EU and how it works. Our disillusionment with our own politicians often comes from the feeling that decisions are being made elsewhere, behind our backs and at a higher level, in some Brussels backroom or on the stock markets of Wall Street. Is this true? What if the decisions that really mattered were being taken by familiar figures such as Angela Merkel, David Cameron, François Hollande and Matteo Renzi, within a set of institutions that act in the name of Europe's citizens but seem to have as their primary purpose the separation of these elites from their own domestic populations?

Writing on the EU has for a long time been the preserve of an elevated caste of scholars, who have developed their own rarefied language to study an object that most of them are very fond of. Many have reproduced the jargon of the Brussels-based institutions without making much effort to translate it. The positive view of the EU held by Europe's political and social elites has meant that few have explored its mysteries and complexities. In Germany, the consensus on all things EU-related has been so complete that the country's public intellectuals have been free to develop the elevated and impenetrable language of legal philosophy to discuss it. In Spain, the association of the EU with the country's cultural and social modernization after the death of Franco has made it an almost irreversible element of Spanish political life and one that is rarely debated.

The aim of this book is to explain the EU without resorting to technical or jargon-laden language. It explains why the EU is so central to political life in Europe but at the same time why it fails to excite us very much. The book punctures two of the most powerful myths of the EU propagated by its supporters and its critics: that it represents a victory over bloody European nationalism and that its bureaucratic weight crushes national democracy in Europe. Neither is true: the mystery of 'ever closer union' is the dilution of political power in the EU by national elites, not the concentration of it in Brussels.

How to read this book

There are different ways to approach this book. Much of it is based on my reading about the European Union over the years and so there are many notes at the end of the book that point to my sources. Given how politically charged the topic of Europe has become, those references are also intended to calm anyone who wonders, as they make their way through the text, 'Where on earth did he get that idea from?' For ease of reading, though, feel free to completely ignore the endnotes.

This book is intended as an introduction to the European Union. I've tried to keep the use of acronyms to a minimum, but some are inescapable. The most confusing is probably the use of the EU, EC and EEC. Are these all referring to the same thing? If not, when did one become the other? There is a chronology at the start of the book which goes some way to answering the question, but let me explain my approach.

I follow a simple rule which reflects the way the EU has developed over time. The European Coal and Steel Community (ECSC) was set up in 1952. What we generally call the Treaty of Rome of 1957 was in fact two treaties: the European Economic Community (EEC) Treaty and the European Atomic Energy Community (Euratom) Treaty. The term European Community (EC) is a simplified way of referring to these three separate communities: the ECSC, the EEC and Euratom. People will sometimes refer to the European Communities, because all three communities were formally bundled together under this plural in 1967. For simplicity, I will stick to the singular. The European Union was founded in 1992 with the signing of the Maastricht Treaty. In 2009, in the Treaty of Lisbon, the term 'European Union' became the official and single name for all these different communities. I will use the term EU whenever I am referring to events after 1992 and EC for anything before that.

There is a final thorny question: can we use 'Europe' as shorthand for the European Union? My general rule is no, as the two things are quite different. On occasion, I will use the term 'Europe' when making a more general and sweeping point. But I believe that, in contrast to the rhetorical flourishes of many of Europe's politicians, the EU has no monopoly on the term 'Europe'.

The book begins with a chapter that focuses on those who rule the EU. It explains how the EU works, but also examines where the power lies. Chapter 2 looks into the origins of the EU. This isn't just a chapter describing one treaty after another; as a process, European integration is bound up with many of the biggest changes that have affected European politics and society since 1945. Chapter 3 asks who wins and who loses from European economic integration and Chapter 4 looks at those who are against the EU. Who are they and what do they want? Chapter 5 is about expansion and it considers the seemingly inexorable rise in the number of European member states, from six in 1952 to twenty-eight today. The last chapter turns to diplomacy: though you might not believe it, the European Union has an elaborate foreign policy. For years, people have been wondering when it will finally make its entrance onto the world stage as a regional superpower.

The conclusion asks perhaps the most important question: is 'ever closer union' compatible with the preservation of democracy at the national level? Europe was the birthplace of democracy, but the relationship between the two has become increasingly fractious. Do we have to choose between the EU and democracy? The book ends on this question. The stakes could not be any higher.

Who Rules Europe?

Europe in five scenes

Scene One: 23 October 2011. The press conference room, in the European Council building in Brussels. French President Nicolas Sarkozy and German Chancellor Angela Merkel brief the press after a summit focusing on the Eurozone economic crisis. Sarkozy is asked by a French journalist whether he was given reassurances by Italian Prime Minister Silvio Berlusconi that Italy would meet its economic reform objectives. Silence. As Sarkozy looks across at Merkel, a cheeky grin breaks out across his face. She looks back, surprised. Then slowly, she gives her own sheepish grin. Journalists in the room guffaw with laughter. As the noise dies down, Sarkozy replies. He has full confidence in the 'entirety of Italy's institutions' and in their ability to implement the reforms. There is no mention of Berlusconi. Less than a month later, Silvio Berlusconi has resigned, putting an end to seventeen years on the front line of Italian politics. We learn later that coordinated efforts to oust him, involving Merkel, Italian President Giorgio Napolitano and leading officials in the European Central Bank (ECB), had existed since the summer of 2011.[1]

Scene Two: 9 June 2014. A glittering lake, in the grounds of the Swedish Prime Minister's summer residence in Harpsund, 120 kilometres south of Stockholm. Four European leaders sit in a small rowing boat, each wearing a life jacket. The leaders are Angela Merkel, Dutch Prime Minister Mark Rutte, British Prime Minister David Cameron and Swedish Prime Minister Fredrik Reinfeldt. As the host, Reinfeldt is doing the rowing. Cameron had said he didn't need a life jacket, claiming that, when it came to swimming, he was 'like a Labrador'. Reinfeldt insisted, saying people had drowned recently in the lake. The occasion is a mini-summit on EU reform. The real purpose of the meeting is to iron out disagreements on the identity of the future President of the European Commission. Pressure from the European Parliament has led to a new procedure, whereby the head of the Commission is decided by the result of the European parliamentary elections. Jean-Claude Juncker was the preferred candidate of the centre-right group in the Parliament, the European People's Party (EPP), and it has won the most votes in the election. David Cameron tries to veto his nomination, believing only heads of government should decide who gets the top job at the European Commission. He marshals his supporters, Rutte and Reinfeldt, in the hope of convincing Merkel to drop her support for Juncker. They fail. A couple of weeks later, at a European Council summit meeting, Juncker's nomination is confirmed. On the margins of that meeting, Finnish Prime Minister Alexander Stubb spoke to journalists. He admitted Juncker might be a bit too federalist for some people in the UK, but, he concluded, the British should 'wake up and smell the coffee'. On 14 July, the same day that the French celebrate the storming of the Bastille, Juncker became the twelfth President of the European Commission. A book written about this new procedure for electing the head of the European Commission describes it as a 'parliamentary putsch', planned from within the corridors of the European Parliament.[2]

Scene Three: 28 June 2015. The towering new European Central Bank headquarters in Frankfurt, Germany. The ECB decides that it will no longer continue providing Greek banks with emergency liquidity assistance. For the past six months, Greek banks had seen huge outflows of cash as Greeks transferred their money overseas. The banks had only survived on the back of the European Central Bank's assistance. When the ECB announced its decision, Greece was forced to declare a bank holiday. From that moment on, for an unspecified period, the banks would be closed and people would only be able to access their accounts via cash machines. A limit of 60 euros a day of withdrawals was imposed. In Athens, long lines formed next to cash machines and Greek pensioners protested outside the closed entrances of the country's banks. When he returned home that day after work, Greek finance minister Yanis Varoufakis breezily told his wife, 'Honey, I shut the banks.'[3]

Scene Four: 13 July 2015, 6 a.m. Brussels. The office of Donald Tusk, President of the European Council. Angela Merkel, Alexis Tsipras and French President François Hollande all sit together in Tusk's office. Tusk is at the head of the table. All other aides and officials have been kept away.

The leaders stretch their tired limbs and push back their chairs. After fourteen hours of negotiations, there is no deal and it is time to accept the possibility that Greece will have to leave the Eurozone. The negotiations had begun two days previously, at a meeting of Eurozone finance ministers. They were there to negotiate an agreement between Greece and its creditors, after Greeks had voted by a large majority on 5 July to reject the terms of the previous bail-out. Tsipras had come to Brussels with what he thought was a strong mandate to negotiate a new deal, but he was met with unwavering resistance. After nine hours of unsuccessful talks, the finance ministers gave up and passed the baton on to their bosses. Negotiations between heads of state and government started on Sunday, the 12th, but by the morning of 13 July there was still no agreement. As the trio of Merkel, Hollande and Tsipras made for the door, Donald Tusk intervened. A tough-talking former football hooligan from Gdansk, Tusk has a reputation for not pulling any punches.[4] 'I'm sorry,' he tells them simply but firmly, 'but there is no way you are leaving this room.' The three leaders go back to discussing the setting up of a controversial 50 billion euro privatization fund, one of the sticking points in the deal. An hour later, they reach a compromise, with the fund to be based in Greece, not in Luxembourg as the German finance minister had hoped. Tusk declares clumsily to a tired press corps: 'One can say that we have "agreekment".'[5]

Scene Five. 24 September 2015, 8 p.m. The main lecture theatre of the Warsaw School of Economics. The event has been organized by the Socialists and Democrats group of the European Parliament. Entitled 'Relaunching Europe', it is intended as a pan-European platform for debate about the future of Europe. In Poland, the local socialist party is weak and there is little interest in an event run by a group of lefties parachuted in from Brussels. The main lecture theatre is virtually empty with the delegation from Brussels outnumbering by a large margin the few students and members of the public in attendance. The event's Twitter feed is projected onto a screen but there are so few tweets that the same messages are continuously recycled one after the other. At the podium is Gianni Pittella, an Italian politician from southern Italy and head of the Socialists and Democrats group. Pittella is giving an impassioned speech about the future of Europe in which he criticizes the 'national egotism' of member states and their slow action over tackling Europe's migration crisis. He says that six months earlier the European Parliament had put together with the European Commission a relocation plan for the refugees. But member states had rejected the plan. Six months later, overwhelmed by the numbers of people arriving on the shores of EU member states, they agree to the original plan. 'Maybe,' Pittella suggests, 'if the member states had decided six months ago, we could have avoided many disasters, many catastrophes.'

Each of these five scenes is drawn from real events. Give or take a bit of poetic licence, they are all true accounts of what happened. However, each of them gives a different answer to the question of who rules Europe. Scene One tells us that leaders of the biggest member states rule over the rest of

Europe, even able to pick and choose their preferred national leaders. Scene Two confirms that national governments rule, but suggests that all of them, even powerful states like the UK, have to be ready to make compromises. Scenes Three, Four and Five suggest that the EU institutions call the shots: they can force the banks to close (Scene Three), they broker the late-night deals (Scene Four) and they make the proposals which governments eventually adopt as their own (Scene Five). How can we make sense of these different ideas of who rules Europe? Do they all have something in common? The rest of this chapter outlines three different visions of the EU that draw on the scenes above and other examples: a Europe of officials, a Europe of peoples and a Europe of states. The unifying theme that runs through all three is discussed in the final section of the chapter: a Europe of secrets.

A Europe of officials

When we think of the EU, we think of its officials. And when we think of its officials, we most often think of the European Commission – the body housed in the star-shaped Berlaymont building, at the heart of the European quarter in Brussels. Empty for thirteen years because of required renovations (prompted by the finding of asbestos), the 'Berlaymonster' has been fully operational since 2004. All twenty-eight European Commissioners are based in the building and their 75-square-metre offices are more than twice the size of an average Parisian apartment (31 square metres). The President, referred to in hushed tones as *'Monsieur le Président'* (there has been no *'Madame la Présidente'* in the organ-

ization's fifty-seven-year history), takes up the entire thir-
teenth floor.

With a staff of just under 25,000 people, the European
Commission is a very small bureaucracy.[6] To put things in
perspective, the British Broadcasting Corporation employs
a staff of just under 19,000 people. A single department of
the federal government in the United States, such as the
Department of Commerce, employs 44,000 people. In
France, 5.6 million people are on the payroll of the French
state; and well over a million people work for the National
Health Service in the UK. Administrative costs associated
with running the Commission take up only 6 per cent of the
EU's budget. National bureaucracies usually account for
between 23 per cent and 28 per cent of a government's
annual budget. That said, the salaries and pensions paid to
European Commission staff are some of the most generous
on offer anywhere. Middle managers, at the AD11 grade, earn
£112,090 a year and pay only 13.4 per cent tax on that.[7] The
European Commission President's annual salary is almost
double that of the French President's and almost four times
that of Spain's Prime Minister.[8]

While the European Commission is not the bureaucratic
monster its critics make it out to be, its role is crucial to the
story of who rules Europe. Under the traditional method of
policy-making in Europe, dubbed the 'Community Method',
the Commission has the sole right to make proposals. These
proposals, if accepted by member states and the European
Parliament, and after an extensive process of redrafting and
scrutinizing, become law. Contrary to conventional wisdom,
the EU's laws are detailed and prescriptive to compensate

for the fact that the Commission has limited powers. Unable to monitor directly the implementation of laws in individual countries, the Commission drafts policies that are as detailed as possible. This is where its reputation for legislating on the size and shape of cucumbers has come from.

The Commission's right of initiative is accompanied by an extensive process of consultation and negotiation. Committees within the European Parliament regularly make suggestions and MEPs are active in sponsoring Commission initiatives, as we saw with the Commission and the Parliament's proposals surrounding refugee quotas. Member states are also a key source of ideas and often ask the Commission for suggestions in a particular area. The European Commission has an obligation to consult with citizens on its policy proposals and is in constant contact with interest groups. Brussels is home to around 30,000 lobbyists, more than the number of people working for the Commission. Wherever drafts of legislation are to be found, lobbyists are there trying to tweak texts in their favour.

Most European laws start their life as a Green Paper drafted by the Commission, on its own initiative or at the request of member states. This paper is circulated widely for comments before entering the EU's legislative machinery. At any one time, there are countless 'non-papers' being passed around the corridors of European institutions. Eventually these will either be discarded or transformed into something more official. It is important to remember that the Commission's powers to propose laws are restricted to those policy areas chosen by member states. As the European Union's activities have expanded into new fields, like police cooperation and financial sector regulation, the Commission's leading role in proposing legislation has been diluted. Angela Merkel has dubbed this shared approach to driving forward the EU's legislative agenda the 'Union Method'.[9]

In a speech in 1977, the newly appointed President of the European Commission, Roy Jenkins, referred to the Commission as a 'citadel': well defended by his predecessors but in desperate need of a new lease of life.[10] The powers of the Commission had been dramatically clipped by de Gaulle in the mid-1960s after the then President of the Commission, Walter Hallstein, had made a bid for more power. From the late 1970s onwards, the Commission's fortunes revived and its heyday was under the rule of the steely French socialist Jacques Delors, who capitalized on a convergence of views between West Germany, France and the United Kingdom to launch an ambitious plan for completing the single market.

Since then, the Commission's fortunes have ebbed once more as power has been transferred to member states and to a new 'grab-bag' of agencies, institutes and new organizations created since the early 1990s.[11] The European Central Bank employed 2,622 staff at the close of 2014 and many of its new powers in financial regulation could conceivably have been vested in the Commission. The External Action Service, set up as part of the European Union's foreign policy, employs 1,628 people and stopped any ambitions the Commission might have had in expanding its remit in foreign affairs. The Commission's monopoly on legislative proposals has been replaced by a much more complex process where ideas and proposals are constantly circulating around the 'Brussels bubble'. A junior official working in the Delors

Commission in the late 1980s would have had more direct influence on policy than a much more senior official working for the European Commission in the early twenty-first century.[12]

A Europe of officials refers to more than just the Commission, however. It points to a common outlook and spirit shared by those actively involved in the EU's policy-making process. It is often the case that national representatives working within the Council have a stronger affinity with their Commission counterparts or with officials from other EU institutions, such as the European Central Bank, than they do with many of their own nationals, in particular those whose work has no connection with the day-to-day affairs of the European Union. An ethos of governing through rules binds all the different actors together. This is as true of the finance ministers in the Eurogroup as it is of the MEPs in their parliamentary committees. This 'European spirit of compromise', as Angela Merkel calls it, is not a commitment to a federal Europe, far from it.[13] Agnostic about how decisions should be taken, it reflects a shared identity born out of the common activity of governing together at the European level. How all of this fits with the competing demands of national democracies is perhaps the trickiest question currently facing the European Union.

A Europe of peoples

Situated between the leafy Leopold Park and the small Luxembourg Square is the sprawling European Parliament complex. The European Parliament resembles a modern-day palace. Its various wings are connected by steel walkways and its reflective windows dazzle passers-by on those rare sunny days in Brussels.

The scale of the building reflects the ambition of the institution. The European Parliament has steadily grown in power ever since direct elections were introduced in 1979. Elections for the 751 members of the European Parliament (MEPs) are held every five years. Since 1992, the Parliament has had co-decision powers, meaning that laws can only be passed with its consent. In 1999, these co-decision powers were expanded and today, under the rules of the Ordinary Legislative Procedure, the Council of Ministers and the European Parliament share the power to assent to laws. Reflecting this increase in power, the Parliament today employs, in addition to its MEPs, almost 6,800 staff. On top of all of this, the European Parliament decamps to its second chamber in Strasbourg once a month, at a cost of around £93 million a year. The origins of this bizarre ritual lie in a French wish to have the Parliament on its own soil. Though efforts have been made to change the rules, not least by the MEPs themselves, the French have dug in their heels.

MEPs have a role in deciding the identity of new Commissioners, though unlike in national political systems, the members of this 'executive' are not drawn from a majority in the European Parliament. Member states nominate individuals and they are vetted and quizzed by MEPs, on the model of US Senate confirmation hearings. In 2014, for the first time, the Parliament was able to connect the results of the May 2014 European elections with the post of the President of the Commission.

Known as the '*Spitzenkandidat*' process (meaning 'top candidate'), this is a rare example of a German (rather than French) word becoming the commonly used term across the rest of Europe.[14] In this process, the main party groups competing in the European elections nominate their 'top candidate' for the presidency of the European Commission. The candidate from the group that wins most seats gets the job. For the first time in 2014 there were presidential-style debates in the run-up to the elections, with the *Spitzenkandidaten* arguing with one another in front of the cameras. The veteran politician Jean-Claude Juncker stood for the centre-right, the former bookseller Martin Schulz stood for the centre-left. The Greens nominated two candidates: the mustachioed and pipe-smoking Frenchman José Bové (famous for attacking a McDonald's restaurant in 1999 in defence of Roquefort cheese) and a young German MEP, Ska Keller. The floppy-haired Belgian federalist Guy Verhofstadt stood for the liberals and the far left was represented by Alexis Tsipras, who became Greek Prime Minister in January 2015. Nine television debates, in three different languages, were held between April and June 2014. Studies show that around 15 per cent of citizens in EU member states watched at least one of the debates, though interest was highest in the countries fielding a candidate.[15]

As the centre-right won the most votes, Juncker was the frontrunner to become the next head of the European Commission. As mentioned earlier, a battle was fought with David Cameron, who believed the authority to nominate the President of the European Commission lay with member states, not with the European Parliament. Cameron lost.

Whether the European Parliament is able to retain this new power will become clear only with the next European elections in 2019.

The statutory powers of the European Parliament have increased steadily since 1979 and since the early 1990s in particular. But does that mean Europe's peoples rule the EU? The reality is more complex and the Parliament's role in this is more ambivalent. A constant difficulty faced by the Parliament has been to match its formal powers with its ability to win support from Europe's populations. Elections for the Parliament since 1979 have seen a steady, almost implacable, decline in turnouts. Indeed, as the powers of the institution have expanded, fewer people have bothered to vote in European elections. In 1979, turnout was 62 per cent. By 1994, it had fallen to just under 57 per cent. Five years later, it was down to below 50 per cent. In 2009 it fell to 43 per cent, and in 2014, in spite of the galvanizing effect expected from the *Spitzenkandidat* process, turnout fell again to 42.54 per cent. Some of the worst turnouts were in the newer member states: in Slovakia, turnout has never reached 20 per cent and in 2014 it fell to its lowest level ever – just over 13 per cent.

This steady decline in turnout raises questions about the legitimacy and the representative capacity of the European Parliament. It has become a central cog in the European Union's legislative machinery but that does not necessarily mean Europe's peoples are better represented than before. The success of the Parliament as an institution does not depend upon its representative capacity. In fact, it may even be the case that in order for the Parliament to be influential in the EU's decision-making, it needs to be *less* representative. We see this most in the co-decision procedures, as they have developed since the late 1990s.

Co-decision refers to the formal obligation for the Parliament and the Council of Ministers to agree on any proposal before it can become law. Being obliged to strike an agreement is not the same thing as being equally and jointly invested in the crafting and designing of European legislation. Most of the detailed policy work takes place in the Council's working groups. Co-decision itself is a strategic process. It is about balancing the interests of the member states with the interests of the European Parliament. Both sides are committed to finding an agreement; the issue is what compromises will be needed in order to achieve it. The interest of the Council, and in particular the country that holds the rotating presidency at any one time, is to get legislation through in line with their agenda. Presidencies often have themes and countries come up with ideas that they want their presidency to be remembered for. The Dutch, who took over the presidency in January 2016, want to tackle the refugee crisis. The Slovaks, who are next in line for the presidency after the Dutch, just want the refugees to go away.[16] The Parliament wants its own mark on the legislation but without bringing the legislative process to a grinding halt.

This concern for efficiency means that policy-making in the EU is surprisingly streamlined. The requirement of co-decision has led the Council, the Commission and the European Parliament to develop procedures to help them work together speedily and effectively. Known as early agreements, these refer to a deal done by the three institutions at the first reading stage: a Commission proposal is agreed before either the Parliament or the Council have adopted formal positions on the proposal.

How can a deal be done so early? On the Parliament's side, draft legislative texts are the preserve of parliamentary committees. These committees are staffed by MEPs who take on the roles of chief rapporteur and shadow rapporteurs. A committee will formulate its position on a legislative proposal and take this into 'trilogue' negotiations, named as such because three institutions are represented: the Commission, the Council and the Parliament. On the Council's side, the trilogue meetings occur before any common position is agreed between member states. The Commission is present in these meetings but is usually quiet. Concerned for the coherence of its proposal, it appreciates that these 'trilogues' are really negotiations between the Council and the Parliament. Trilogue discussions are dominated by matters of process – how to get an agreement in order to pass this piece of legislation – rather than debating the merits of any particular law.

In the 1999–2004 term of the European Parliament, 28 per cent of legislation was passed at first reading. This percentage rose to 72 per cent in the 2004–9 term. Between 2009 and 2013, 81 per cent of proposals were passed at first reading via the trilogue method. Only 3 per cent ever reached third reading, which is where texts are debated in plenary sessions of the Parliament. The dilemma for the European Parliament is clear. If it wants to be an efficient participant in these trilogues, it has to be united as an institution and give full backing to its rapporteurs in their negotiations with the Council.

But a fully representative Parliament would surely reveal that European populations do not have a single view on any particular topic. European societies are made up of multiple and overlapping conflicts between old and young, rich and poor, urban and rural, North and South, East and West. If the Parliament is to remain a key player, none of these deep divisions can imprint themselves on the EU's legislative process. In national politics, these sorts of disagreements have been the basis for the formation of political parties and national party systems. Forced to choose between its representativeness and its institutional influence within the EU, and lacking the kind of pan-European political parties that would translate Europe's multiple divisions into identifiable rival programmes, the Parliament has repeatedly chosen to maximize its influence by being as unified as possible. The Parliament may play a role in ruling the EU but that doesn't mean Europe's peoples do as well.

A Europe of states

Europe has to serve all twenty-eight countries,
not just one.
MATTEO RENZI[17]

In the final analysis, the European Union is ruled by its member states. Policies that don't have the support of member states are filed away. Some lip service may be paid to them but they rarely see the light of day. Take the *Five Presidents' Report* on the future of the Eurozone, published in June 2015, most noteworthy for revealing how many people there are in Brussels with the title of 'President'. The signatories are Jean-Claude Juncker, President of the European Commission, Martin Schulz, President of the European Parliament, Jeroen Dijsselbloem, President of the Eurogroup, Donald Tusk, President of the European Council, and Mario Draghi, President of the European Central Bank. When the report was launched, there was no fanfare, no media storm and no photo with the five presidents standing together brandishing their report. Member states eventually discussed it in October 2015. They 'took stock' of the report but without endorsing any of its recommendations about how to integrate the Eurozone further.[18] Without the political will of member states, proposals go nowhere, even those produced by some of the most powerful men in Europe. Federalist and Eurosceptic politicians systematically deny this fact about the European Union: both prefer to believe that the European Union is ruled by its supranational institutions, benignly in the eyes of the federalists and malignly in the eyes of the Eurosceptics.

The body which gives the European Union its sense of direction and sets its medium- to long-term goals is the European Council. This institution dates back to December 1974 when a decision was taken at a summit in Paris to transform regular meetings of heads of government into a European Council.[19] This idea came from the then French President, Valéry Giscard d'Estaing, who proposed it to the German Chancellor Helmut Schmidt, as a way of circumventing the slow and complex decision-making procedures of the European Community. At the time, there were far fewer members of the EC than there are today (after the British,

Irish and Danish entries in 1973, there were nine members). The meetings of the European Council were intimate affairs made up of fireside chats and extensive amounts of cigar smoke. Leaders were able to have long conversations unburdened by protocol and hidden from the glare of public scrutiny.

Since those early days, the European Council has been transformed. Its power has grown along with its formal status as an official institution of the European Union. The intimacy is not entirely lost, though, as the scene where Tusk brought Tsipras, Hollande and Merkel together to hammer out a deal on Greece's bail-out suggests. The European Council meetings have plenary sessions, accompanied by 'bilaterals' in which the President of the European Council tries to eliminate sticking points in têtes-à-têtes with national leaders. The cigar smoke, however, has disappeared.

Today, the European Council is not only responsible for giving Europe a strategic direction, it is also involved in many day-to-day aspects of EU affairs, particularly when there are crises to be managed. It has been at the centre of the Eurozone economic crisis and the more recent refugee crisis. In order to hammer out urgent deals, its bi-monthly meetings have been supplemented with ad hoc crisis-summits. The European Council is where the British Prime Minister had to seal his renegotiation with the EU on UK membership, with the calendar of the referendum timed with the meetings of the European Council.

Below the European Council is the Council of Ministers. Officially, though confusingly, the latter institution is known as 'the Council' whereas the European Council is known as 'the Council of the European Union'. Still reading? Good. The Council of Ministers has the responsibility of both making and passing laws. It is a pyramid structure, with working groups at the bottom, committees of senior national ambassadors higher up, and ministers from national governments at the top. The Council is organized by policy area with less-than-imaginative titles: finance ministers meet in a body called 'Ecofin', ministers of agriculture and fisheries meet in 'Agrifish' and so on.

The working groups are also organized thematically and work on specific legislative proposals. They are staffed by national experts who are the starting point for any negotiations around a particular text. This is why they are also known as 'preparatory bodies'. These experts identify any national conflicts in terms of the acceptability and implementation of a proposed law and then find viable solutions, scrutinizing and reworking proposals, thus playing an important role in the crafting of European legislation. Today, there are around 300 working groups that account for much of the regular traffic between Brussels and national capitals.

Remaining disagreements are passed up the pyramid structure to the national ambassadors who sit on the Committee of Permanent Representatives (Coreper). This committee is divided into two, Coreper I and Coreper II. The latter is responsible for the most politically controversial and sensitive policy areas, such as economic and financial affairs. Coreper is a crucial part of the Council structure. Disagreements that cannot be solved by Coreper have to go onto the busy agendas of national ministers when they meet in their various Council configurations. Too many disagreements make these meetings impossible to run, especially today with twenty-eight member states of the EU. They also make for bad headlines back home if a minister ends up outvoted on a proposal.

Formally, there must always be a vote by 'qualified majority' in the Council of Ministers and disagreements within the Council have increased in recent years. That said, the preference is overwhelmingly for decisions made by consensus. The UK, one of the most truculent of member states, was in a losing minority only 12 per cent of the time over the 2009–15 period. Other member states were very infrequently, or almost never, in such a position.[20] The success of Coreper is judged by how few contentious issues reach the tables of government ministers. Those who sit on Coreper are seasoned Brussels insiders who represent their member states but are based in the Belgian capital. They run the often large permanent representations of the member states in Brussels and usually know each other very well. Not only are they committed to representing their governments' interests, they also want to keep the European show on the road. And they do a pretty good job of this: around 70 per cent of the legislation reaching ministers has already been agreed upon and needs only a political thumbs-up to become law.

The Council has its own army of officials whose role is to make sure that the coordinated activity of member states runs smoothly. These officials are collectively known as the General Secretariat of the Council. As well as providing secretarial assistance to member states, these officials have their own expertise. The importance of the General Secretariat is greatest when there is a small country holding the rotating presidency of the Council. This presidency changes hands every six months and the General Secretariat provides continuity amid all of this change. Some large states, like France or Italy, have extensive diplomatic machines that manage the rotating presidency well. Smaller states rely on the General Secretariat for logistical help and for advice on drawing up the Council's agenda.

All of this elaborate institutional machinery is designed to facilitate common decision-making by member states. These decisions are based on texts which they have helped to draft, scrutinize and shape at every stage. Member states don't always agree and sometimes they are out-voted in the Council. One of the British government's greatest fears is that as more and more members of the EU join the Eurozone, they will find themselves out-voted in the Council by a powerful Eurozone bloc of countries. As we saw in Scene Two, Cameron was on the losing side in his campaign to stop Jean-Claude Juncker from becoming President of the European Commission. When governments finally adopted a proposal for sharing out refugees, it was done against the wishes of Romania, the Czech Republic, Hungary and Slovakia. Prime Minister of Slovakia Robert Fico had originally agreal to take only 200 refugees, 'preferably Christians'. He has since promised to ignore the mandatory resettlement policy voted on in September 2015.

In spite of this search for consensus, traditional forms of power matter for the decisions taken by Europe's member states. If Europe is ruled by its member states, it may not be ruled by all of them in equal measure. In the past, figures such as General de Gaulle threw their weight around in Europe, making it clear that its institutions were there to serve and enhance French power. More recently, it has become commonplace to say that we live in a 'German Europe', where Germany calls the shots and all other member states have to follow. Does this mean that Europe is ruled by its most powerful and economically successful member state?

Germany's influence in Europe is enormous. In three of our opening scenes, Angela Merkel takes centre-stage. When finance ministers of the Eurogroup meet, few pay much attention to the speech given by the Latvian or Slovenian representative. But when the German finance minister speaks, everyone listens.[21] European diplomats will confirm that a policy is only really 'on the table' if the Germans are in favour of it. If not, it's dead in the water. Angela Merkel has been in power in Germany since 2005 and she is widely known as the 'Chancellor of Europe'. Reportedly, even the French are in awe of her. After a meeting with former French President Nicolas Sarkozy during the euro crisis, an amused Merkel told a group of journalists that during the whole meeting, Sarkozy's foot had been nervously jiggling up and down.[22]

This fashionable view exaggerates the role of Germany, confusing German hegemony over the rest of Europe with two rather different things. One is the unquestioned dominance of Angela Merkel over domestic German politics. She rose to power by pushing aside the country's leading alpha males – Helmut Kohl, Gerhard Schröder and Joschka Fischer. Merkel's red-black coalition (that combines her own centre-right party with the centre-left Social Democrats) has 80 per cent of the seats in the German Bundestag. The only real opposition is Die Linke, a left-wing party with 10 per cent of the seats. In many Bundestag debates, Merkel ignores the strident rhetoric of Die Linke leader Sahra Wagenknecht, preferring instead to chat with colleagues or stare into space.[23]

People are fascinated by the combination of Merkel's ruthless pursuit of power and her aversion to the macho rhetoric of Germany's predominantly male political class. She hates public speaking and lacks charisma. She is cautious and without any obvious political vision, and yet she has managed to win over a Christian Democratic party heavily influenced by southern Bavarian Catholics who have never thought of Merkel as 'one of them'. After her most audacious move ever, the welcoming of Syrian refugees to Germany, members of her party (including her own finance minister) started to criticize her publicly. But at the annual Christian Democrat Party conference in Karlsruhe in December 2015, she was given a nine-minute standing ovation.

Because Merkel's power is so complete within Germany, she appears to the rest of Europe as a towering figure. Germany's economic weight and demography are such that the country will always play a leading role in Europe. It accounts for 21 per cent of the EU's total GDP and has the highest population by some margin. But this power lacks any conscious project of domination. A large majority of Germans remain highly sceptical of playing a greater role in international affairs. When Russia invaded the Crimea in 2014, sparking a war between eastern separatists and the Ukrainian government in Kiev, the response in Germany was a mixture of indifference and anxiety.[24] Germans did not want to be disturbed or embroiled in a far-off conflict. Merkel's intransigence over renegotiating Greece's terms with its creditors does not stem from a desire to humiliate Greece or to suck dry its few remaining economic assets. Merkel views Germany as vulnerable: an ageing population with a low birth rate should not incur large debts. Fiscal prudence is driven by an assessment of the internal weaknesses of the German model. A fascination with Angela Merkel's domestic political supremacy has mistakenly spilt over into a belief that she rules Europe.

Another reason for this confusion about Germany's role in Europe is that it has coincided with a weakening of the European Union's supranational institutions. These are the bodies that are meant to represent the European interest as a whole. Big and small states are members of the European Union but through these supranational institutions their differences of size and clout are flattened out. When Commissioners are appointed in the European Commission, they promise to leave their national interests behind and work for the common European good. This is why small states like Ireland or Austria place great hopes in them. However, over the last couple of decades, supranational institutions have become weaker. Governments have become wary of delegating more powers to them in case there is a public backlash, preferring instead to create new independent agencies.[25] As the supranational varnish of the European Union wears off, we see more clearly the power of the big states lying underneath. And Germany is the big state that we focus on more than any other. The appearance of a so-called

German Europe is in fact the retreat over time of the European Union's supranational institutions. One should not be confused with the other.

A Europe of secrets

A common thread connects all of these different visions of who rules Europe. The trilogues of the Council and the Parliament, the consultations of the European Commission, the intensive deliberations of the European Council in moments of tension and crisis – all are bound by the common thread of secrecy. Decision-making in Europe is done over-whelmingly behind closed doors. Exactly who is taking the decisions is perhaps less important than the fact that, whoever it is, it is being done with a minimum of public visibility.

We see this when we consider the rationale behind the EU's institutions. The European Council is attractive as a venue for heads of state and government because it is a place where leaders can discuss with one another with far less protocol and without any fear of having their remarks published in the European press. Even when they do have to meet in a more formal setting, their accompanying national delegations are consigned to a different room. The only ones allowed into the European Council meetings are the institution's top diplomats, known as the Council 'Antici'. The title Antici comes from the name of the Italian diplomat who invented this system in the 1970s. The role of these Antici diplomats is to take notes. Every fifteen minutes, one of them leaves the room where the politicians are and goes to another room where all the national Antici diplomats are sat together. The diplomat from the Council reads his notes, and the national diplomats take their own notes. This relaying of information goes on for the duration of the meeting. If there is some sort of emergency in the talks, the national Antici diplomats have access to a phone with which they can reach their own national delegations. The notes taken down by the national Antici diplomats make up what is known as the Antici protocols. These are strictly secret documents, very rarely leaked to the press. However, even if they are leaked, they are not direct notes of the European Council meetings, only hearsay. The only written transcripts that exist of the European Council meetings are the result of this bizarre form of Chinese whispers.

The Council of Ministers shares this attachment to secrecy.[26] While the Council has a clear legislative function, as we saw above, it is also a place of deliberation and bargaining between national representatives. We are accustomed to diplomatic negotiations being conducted in secret, but not common legislative business. Notwithstanding its central legislative role, the Council has opted for privacy. The specific rules adopted by the Council regarding secrecy take rules normally applied to foreign policy and apply them to all its business, which is overwhelmingly directed at the sorts of domestic issues that in the past have been the preserve of national legislatures.[27] The result, in the words of the British historian Perry Anderson, is to 'convert the open agenda of parliaments into the closed world of chancelleries'.[28]

For those involved, the usefulness of the working groups and the Coreper committees consists in their place outside the limelight. When finance ministers arrive in Brussels for meetings of Ecofin, the Brussels press corps is waiting for them. Briefings are given before and after and, if something particularly important is known to be on the agenda, then there are expectations about what will be said and agreed. In contrast, the working groups and Coreper excite no interest. They carry out routine activities that lack the political spice that makes for good news stories. For that reason, they get on with the bulk of the European Union's legislative business unimpeded. Even then, what actually happens inside Ecofin and the other ministerial councils is only known to the participants. The videos of Council activities are classified under 'doorsteps', 'roundtables' and 'statements'. The actual deliberations and negotiations are secret.

The 'trilogue' and early agreement system, now the norm in the EU's Ordinary Legislative Procedure, are distinguished by their attachment to 'secluded' decision-making.[29] Trilogues are as far removed from the public deliberations typical of legislative chambers as one can imagine. Only when texts reach the third reading are they really debated in plenaries, with the political partisanship of the MEPs driving the debates. Only a fraction of draft laws ever reach that stage. The legislative life of the EU is centred around small and select clusters of people, representing their respective institutions, meeting behind closed doors and hammering out agreements that both sides can be happy with. It is no coincidence that the Parliament's greatest triumph, the *Spitzenkandidat* process, was the result of a behind-the-scenes *coup d'état* planned and carried out by a select few parliamentarians. That is one reason it had no discernible effect on raising the turnout at European elections.

Conclusion

The member states are at the heart of the European Union. The notion that sovereignty has been sucked out of the nation-state and recast at the European level, so popular among Eurosceptics like Marine Le Pen and Nigel Farage, makes a nonsense of how the EU is actually run. More than anything else, the EU involves the close cooperation of many thousands of national officials and politicians in a shared project of law-making at the European level. Looking closely at where European law comes from, we see that the Commission's right of initiative is only relative. Many proposals originate in suggestions by member states and the real scrutiny and redrafting of laws takes place within the Council of Ministers, the legislative heart of the EU. The European Parliament's input is significant but its interest is above all in the process by which laws are agreed. The Parliament is a strategic actor more than it is a law-maker.

To say that member states rule Europe is, however, a little misleading. It begs the question of what exactly we mean by member states. We saw that Europe's peoples do not rule through the Parliament as this institution has sacrificed its representative role in favour of being an influential insider in the EU's legislative machine. Do the people rule Europe indirectly through the involvement of their own governments in EU decision-making? A Europe ruled by its member states is a Europe ruled by national executives and an army of civil servants, some based in national capitals, some based in Brussels, and some employed by supranational institutions such as the

European Commission. What makes this system work is its insulation from the controversies and competing demands of national politics. The vast majority of those involved in EU policy-making believe in the need for compromise and the search for consensus. This implies a degree of flexibility and pragmatism that sits uneasily with the need to represent the interests of a domestic population. The virtue of the EU for national politicians and officials is the freedom it gives to them to discuss with one another, unencumbered by their domestic publics. In order to maintain that freedom, much of what the EU does takes place behind closed doors.

Europe today exists as two spheres connected to one another in principle but drifting apart in practice. On the one side are Europe's governments, leaders, ministers, diplomats and civil servants. Together with the small numbers of officials employed directly by the EU's institutions, this sphere is the 'Brussels bubble'. It does not exist separately from Europe's member states, it *is* those member states. On the other side are Europe's populations, the continent's national political parties and its many national legislatures. The political and social life of Europe's many peoples has been cast adrift by the European Union. The appearance of the EU as standing alone and separately from its member states is really a reflection of the growing distance between governments and their own societies in Europe.

Where Did the European Union Come From?

Europe always has been and always will be a pile of little countries thrown together higgledy-piggledy which'll fight tooth and nail for their own national specialities, for their spaghetti, for their Pale-Ale, for their Goethe.

HUGO CLAUS, *THE SORROW OF BELGIUM*, 1994

Historians of European integration are faced with the difficulty of spinning a single story out of the incredible diversity of national experiences of European integration. Where you stand on what the EU is and where it has come from depends a lot on where in Europe you are sitting and where you have been sitting for the past seventy years. A German understanding of European integration reflects the country's preoccupation with the control and limitation of power. Europe is defined in terms of rules and institutions that take the sting out of national interests. German federalism is for Germans a good starting point and the celebrated Basic Law – as the 1949 constitution of West Germany was called – is seen as a model for a constitutional arrangement at the European level.

An Italian, Spanish or Greek understanding of the EU is less about the limiting of power. For these countries, the European Union has provided an alternative to their own venal political class, in thrall to shipping magnates, the mafia and other shadowy private interests. The slogan in Spain when the country joined the Common Market in 1986 was a phrase taken from the work of the Spanish philosopher José Ortega y Gasset: 'Spain is the problem, Europe the solution.'

From a British or a Danish perspective, the EU is understood as a more voluntary affair, a 'partnership' of equals in which further steps towards integration are matters of choice. Behind this vision lies the original assumption made by Winston Churchill, who, in a famous speech about a 'United States of Europe' in Zurich in September 1946, assumed that Britain and its empire would sit comfortably alongside this new federal construction, on friendly terms with it but on no account a member of it. Nicholas Ridley, a minister in Margaret Thatcher's Cabinet, once defined Europe rather more crudely, as 'a German racket'.[1] While the Eastern European view of the European Union focuses on growth and material prosperity, there are also parallels with the German view. During the accession process in the late 1990s and early 2000s, when many feared a backlash against the effects of post-communist transition, being part of the European Union was seen as a way of protecting Eastern European states from themselves.[2] This has occurred again recently, with liberals in Hungary and Poland seeing the power of Brussels as the only way of taming their nationalist leaders.

Historians of the EU have often simplified the past in the search for a guiding thread to their narratives. We are regularly told that the roots of the EU lie in the rubble and human misery of the Second World War. Under the slogan 'Never again', far-sighted diplomats such as Robert Schuman, Jean Monnet and Paul-Henri Spaak pushed Europe towards cooperation rather than conflict. When the European Union was awarded the Nobel Peace Prize in 2012, it was for the 'advancement of peace and reconciliation, democracy and human rights' in Europe over six decades. For historians writing in this vein, there is something inevitable about 'ever closer union': its development is associated with progress in the way that Whig historians saw in the rise of political liberty a move from darkness to light. A Christian theme of redemption echoes around these histories. Richard Mayne, a passionate British federalist and key player in the early years of the EC, called his book on European integration *The Recovery of Europe* (1970), with the telling subtitle 'From Devastation to Unity'. Konrad Jarausch's recent work on Europe in the twentieth century is dramatically entitled *Out of Ashes*. This view of European integration as something implacable and unquestionably positive is reflected in many academic theories. A key concept in analysing integration is 'spill-over', the idea that integration in one area can – by accident as much as by design – lead to integration in another area.

This chapter argues that national diversity does not make a history of European integration impossible. Common threads can be found, without having to resort to excessive simplification. The romantic histories of European integration – what the British historian Alan Milward dismissively labelled 'federalist fables' – capture an important part of what people felt in the period immediately after the Second World War. The desire to prevent further conflict combined with a firm belief that responsibility for war lay with Europe's nation-states. The problem with these histories is that they miss the complexity of Europe's development since 1945. They exaggerate the role of 'Europe' as a political project in early post-war European politics and they stress continuity at the expense of change. The effortless move from ECSC to EEC to EC and then finally to EU may suggest that 'ever closer union' is just one long and drawn-out process, punctured only by the odd crisis or two. The reality is quite different.

There are two histories of European integration. The European Union of the twenty-first century is only very distantly related to the post-war years of the 1940s and 1950s. Europe at that time was shaped by a desire for security and stability after years of fighting. People wanted economic growth and an end to the privations of the war years. Once the European economy was booming, measures were needed to manage the pressures arising from rapid economic expansion, which is what integration in the 1950s was all about. The EU of the 1990s and 2000s is a very different animal and a product of other historical forces. It owes its existence to the crisis of Europe's post-war 'Golden Age' of growth and the way this crisis transformed European states and societies. Prosperity and confidence gave way to spiralling inflation, unemployment and a loss of direction for Europe's political classes. It was the response to this crisis by Europe's governments, and in particular their efforts at isolating themselves from the demands and expectations of their own societies, that laid the foundation for today's EU.

Sovereignty destroyed

At the beginning of Elio Vittorini's powerful 1949 novel *Women of Messina*, post-war Italy is described as a country of nomads and wanderers. People travel from one end of the country to another, looking for loved ones or seeking a place where they can start a new life. The novel is about a group of people who respond to the absence of state authority by organizing themselves into a cooperative. Tension builds up as the government reasserts itself, absorbing this group into the officialdom of the reconstructed Italian state. The dissolution of state authority during the war and its speedy reimposition in peacetime was a common theme in European literature at the time. One of Doris Lessing's characters in her short story 'The Other Woman', set in post-war Britain, refers to the army of social security workers created by the Labour government as 'nosy parkers': people wanting to know – without a good cause – other people's business.

The Second World War had exposed the fragility of national sovereignty as an organizing principle of social and political life. The French political right quickly caved in to German pressure. The slogan 'rather Hitler than Blum' revealed the depth of their hostility to the Jewish socialist Léon Blum, who had led the Popular Front government before the war. In Eastern Europe, the destruction of sovereignty was even more complete. Czechoslovakia was cynically sacrificed by Western powers at Munich in 1938. On 6 October 1939 Poland capitulated and was promptly divided up between Germany and the USSR. Soviet foreign minister Molotov declared that Poland had 'ceased to exist'. By the end of the war, a quarter of the country's population had been killed or banished and the country's intelligentsia and propertied classes had been decimated.[3] When the Soviets took over after the war, they filled the vacuum left by the departing Wehrmacht troops.

People had not expected the European state system to survive. At the height of Germany's western offensive, when Charles de Gaulle had retreated to London, members of his entourage put forward plans for an Anglo-French Union. This included common citizenship and a common executive. Winston Churchill presented the idea to the British Cabinet in June 1940 and it was met with agreement. It was the French who rejected it, preferring to make their peace with Hitler. Federalism had become common currency in many political circles in Europe. Though Hitler despised the European unity movement, he was not averse to presenting his plans for continental hegemony in the language of a New European Order. On the left, federalism was embraced by former communists like Altiero Spinelli, who smuggled out from his prison on the island of Ventotene a federalist 'manifesto' which was then taken up by the Italian resistance movement. He went on to create the Union of European Federalists in Paris in December 1946, but soon found himself swimming against the tide as the post-war European order took shape.

Sovereignty reborn

The great surprise of the post-war period was the speed with which the nation-state was resurrected. Only a few years after the war, people were once again living within the ordered European state system that they had known before 1939.[4] Exiled leaders returned to take up their vacant posts.

The Dutch Queen Wilhelmina was welcomed back to the Netherlands and the country's constitutional monarchy was tidily restored. Leopold III of Belgium had a more difficult time, but mainly because he married his governess without asking the permission of his ministers. In these small states, populations knew they had been too weak to resist Nazi rule and they seized the opportunity to re-establish the political status quo ante.[5] The stability of this familiar political framework gave Belgian bankers and Dutch capitalists the confidence to cooperate with one another, which was the foundation for the Benelux treaty of 1948.[6] Guidance was provided by elder statesmen, like de Gaulle and Alcide de Gasperi, figures associated with the past. Konrad Adenauer's nickname was *Der Alte*, the old man.

How do we explain this embrace of the nation-state framework after sovereignty had been so decisively destroyed during the war years? After 1945, people wanted economic security and the target of their demands was their own governments. In Britain, Winston Churchill was seen as a great leader who had led the country to victory, but also as an out-of-touch aristocrat. Voters turned instead to Clement Attlee's Labour Party in the 1945 general election. Three years later the National Health Service was created. A similar change in public opinion was felt across Western Europe, with the economist Friedrich Hayek lamenting in 1943 that politicians were 'in some measure all socialists'.[7] The old Catholic parties, rebranded Christian Democrats in a bid to cross the confessional divide, shifted noticeably to the left. The force with which people across Europe demanded a better life for themselves revived the nation-state. Warfare states were replaced with welfare states across the western half of the continent.[8]

What made all of this possible was a class compromise. During the war the political left had accepted the nationalist war aims of the Allied governments. The French Communist leader, Maurice Thorez, in a speech in 1945 at Waziers in northern France, told his audience of coalminers that producing more was an elevated form of class duty. The First World War, in contrast, had radicalized the left. The war effort had been seen as an upper-class cause pursued at the expense of working-class lives. This radicalism burst forth in revolutions – in Russia in 1917, in Hungary and Germany in 1919 – that shook the capitalist system. Nothing similar happened after 1945. Instead, the conflict between capitalism and democracy – so violent and unceasing in the first half of the twentieth century – was resolved through a compromise between business and labour.

The fruit of this compromise was the welfare state. The era of social security, state-guaranteed pensions, paid vacations and subsidized housing had come. The post-war era witnessed extensive state involvement in national economic life and widespread efforts at national planning. France, Britain, Italy, Sweden, Norway, the Netherlands, Belgium and Austria all launched their own ambitious plans for economic modernization. This required nationalization, with the British government taking control of the Bank of England, the coal industry and the railways. In France, the government seized the assets of Renault, the car company whose founder had been accused of collaboration with the Nazis. In Sweden, the government launched a 'one million apartment programme', a promise to build 100,000 apartments a year for ten years to meet the rising demand for housing.[9] This new era of state planning in Western Europe shared the same goals as the Soviets: to raise the productive potential of key sectors of the economy.[10]

Europe's coal and steel cartel

European integration began with the establishment of the Coal and Steel Community in 1952. This may not seem the most obvious place to start, given the ambitious plans developed by European federalists before and during the war. But European integration in this period was about strengthening, not overcoming, the nation-state. The mining of coal and the making of steel were key industries in post-war Europe. In the late 1940s and 1950s, before the widespread use of oil, steel was fired by coal. Steel production in France was dependent upon access to the coal mines of western Germany. France's modernization plans had assumed this access would be guaranteed, but there was no mechanism for achieving it. Another problem was foreign competition. Non-European and American producers of steel were a threat to both Germany and France. The United States alone accounted for half of world industrial production.

Security considerations also played a part in the formation of the Coal and Steel Community. The concern in Washington at the escalating Cold War with Soviet Russia provided a strong rationale for continued American economic support to Western Europe. It is also true that these industries were associated with militarism and placing their management in the hands of an independent body, known as the High Authority, seemed one way of making war between France and Germany less likely in the future. However, the European Coal and Steel Community is probably best understood as a cartel. The French needed it most and the West Germans accepted it as a way of ending their post-war isolation. Both sides were concerned with the modernization of these industries, as were the governments of the Benelux states, the Belgians in particular. Modernization would come at a cost and the High Authority was designed as a tool for dealing with the social fall-out. The Schuman declaration of 1950 outlined plans for a 'restructuring fund' that would offset the hardship produced by re-establishing the coal and steel industries on a wider European basis. For this reason, some politicians dismissed the High Authority as a socialist instrument. Belgian politicians accused it of leading to a backdoor nationalization of the Belgian coal industry.

The European Coal and Steel Community (ECSC) fitted perfectly with the bigger ambition of building welfare states after the war. It chimed with the goals of social democracy and the economic doctrine of Keynesian demand management. By the late 1950s, however, the ECSC had been overtaken by events. The Korean War (1950–53) had raised demand for steel and made the modernization of these industries less urgent. Buoyant economic growth, which boosted trade between Western European economies, helped maintain demand as well. By the time Western European governments came together for the next step in integration, the Coal and Steel Community had lost much of its relevance.[11]

Managing the good times

By the mid-1950s, much of Western Europe was booming. In 1954, rationing of meat and bacon finally ended in the UK; in France the 'Club Med' era of fashionable all-inclusive holiday resorts was around the corner and car sales were starting to rise.[12] The good times had arrived. They came with their own problems, however. Rapidly growing economies are often associated with rising price levels. This means imports become cheaper than goods made at home and countries suffer repeated balance of payments problems. This was the experience of the British economy in particular, which was hobbled by balance of payment crises throughout the 1950s and 1960s.

The Treaty of Rome, signed in 1957 by the leaders of France, West Germany, Italy, Belgium, the Netherlands and Luxembourg, was designed to solve some of these problems. By creating a common external tariff, member countries of the new European Economic Community (EEC) were able to raise the prices of imports and stem their balance of payments problems. A common external tariff had support from many different groups because of the ubiquity of very high rates of post-war growth. As a whole, the period 1950–73 saw growth rates far higher than any Western European economies have seen since.

As we will see in the next chapter, there is some debate about whether this customs union fuelled economic growth

	1950–73	1973–95	1995–2003
Netherlands	4.4	2.0	0.6
United Kingdom	2.9	2.4	1.8
Denmark	4.1	1.7	1.7
West Germany	6.0	2.7	1.9
France	5.1	2.7	1.3
Italy	5.1	2.5	0.5
Austria	5.9	2.3	2.3
Spain	6.2	3.6	-0.3
Greece	6.4	1.7	3.1
Portugal	6.7	2.0	1.6

Table 2.1

Economic Growth in Western Europe (as % of Gross Domestic Product)

Source: Crafts, 2003.[13] The figures for West Germany in 1995-2003 refer to a reunified Germany.

in Europe at this time. Economists have tended to see it as the other way around – with growth driving trade. What is clear, though, is that the Treaty of Rome of 1957 was bound up with the pressures and challenges of Europe's post-war 'Golden Age' of growth and rising prosperity.

Welfare for farmers

The connection between this phase of European integration and the building of the welfare state is most obvious in the assistance the EC provided to farmers and peasants. The Common Agricultural Policy (CAP) was part of the Treaty of Rome, though the policy was only put into practice a few years later. It became famous for its 'butter mountains' and 'wine lakes', as farmers were increasingly being paid to produce goods for which there was no real market. Part of the problem was that the CAP had little to do with trade in foodstuffs. It was essentially an extension of the principles of the welfare state to farmers.[14]

Europe had long suffered from the problem of rural poverty. Farmers and rural labourers had turned in large numbers to fascism in the inter-war period as an answer to their troubles. Supporting agricultural incomes was a way to avoid a return to inter-war radicalism. There was also a strong whiff of post-war conservatism in the decision to set up the Common Agricultural Policy. Governments promoted the land and the countryside – what the French call *le terroir* – as a core part of a country's national identity. Farming representatives played this trump card in their active lobbying of governments.

The signatories of the Rome treaty wanted to include agricultural goods within the common market, even though providing for their own farmers violated the principle of non-discrimination. The squaring of the circle was achieved by arranging support for farmers on a Community-wide basis. As Chapter 4 explains, an irony of the Common Agricultural Policy is that, in spite of its key function as a source of welfare for farmers, it has ended up helping most those who need it least, namely Europe's biggest landowners.

The national limits to Europe

This first phase of European integration remained small in scale and limited in scope. One of the main architects of the Treaty of Rome, the Belgian Paul-Henri Spaak, noted in his memoirs that most people were not hostile to this idea of closer European cooperation, they were 'merely indifferent'.[15] At the time, people's attention was on their own governments and on the opportunities provided to them by their growing economies.

Because of this, more ambitious attempts in the early 1950s to build a European army came to nothing. An increasingly heated public debate in France ended in 1954 with a rejection of the European Defence Community in the French national assembly. When the result was announced, Gaullists and Communists linked arms and joyfully sang 'La Marseillaise'. The role of Charles de Gaulle in bringing European integration to a standstill made him into a bête noire for pro-Europeans. Twice he torpedoed British hopes of joining the

European Community. He was also behind the 'empty chair crisis', which saw the removal of the French representative from the Council of Ministers in 1965. This was in opposition to efforts by the European Commission to expand its budgetary powers.

For all of his idiosyncrasies, de Gaulle embodied a more general trend. Those so hopeful about the prospects for European integration in the early 1950s had not accounted for the staying power of national sentiment. From the East Indies to Algeria, European empires collapsed. As a result, nationalists held on more desperately than ever to the nation-state. De Gaulle's decision to retain full control over the French nuclear deterrent was a message of support to a French military establishment still smarting over the loss of Algeria. Elsewhere, the collapse of empire focused attention on securing the benefits of the economic miracle. The Dutch East Indies had been described as the 'cork which keeps the Dutch economy from sinking'. Dutch politicians had believed the loss of their empire would – God forbid – bring the Netherlands down to the level of its neighbour, Denmark.[16] The Dutch fought a draining campaign in the late 1940s which ended with Indonesian independence in 1949. After that, the imperial question fell out of favour. The Dutch devoted themselves, with characteristic success, to the pursuit of national economic growth.

After the war, people wanted a better life for themselves and their children. It was to their own governments that they turned, not to an abstract notion of 'Europe'. This kept European integration in the background, as one of many developments after the war and by no means the most important one.

The good times come to an end

Historians of European integration have labelled the 1970s a decade of 'euro-sclerosis'. It was not a period of complete stagnation. The European Community expanded its membership in 1973 with the entry of the United Kingdom, Ireland and Denmark. Cooperation in foreign policy began under the enigmatic heading of 'European Political Cooperation'. After the collapse of the Bretton Woods system, which had managed the currencies of advanced economies since the end of the war, a European arrangement for the coordination of exchange rates was set up. Known as the 'snake', national currencies were pegged to one another and allowed to move only within a strict set of upper and lower limits. Those who believe in the perseverance of the 'European idea' see the late 1960s and 1970s as a blip, a hiatus in the forward march of European integration. It would be more accurate to say that by the mid-1960s the first phase of European integration had exhausted itself, overtaken by more powerful and pressing events. The decade of the 1970s is the occasion of a recasting of the European project altogether.

Many expected the dissolution of the EC in the 1970s and there was much guesswork as to who would leave first. The British decision to join reflected the desperate plight of the UK economy more than any vitality on the part of the EC. A former Belgian Prime Minister, Leo Tindemans, dubbed 'Mr Europe' by his fans, was asked in 1974 to write a report on the meaning of 'European union'. Though he recommended building a 'citizen's Europe', the report was notable for the dark mood, similar to the one that prevails today in Brussels. Tindemans warned that 'the Community is crumbling beneath the resurgence, which is felt everywhere, of purely national preoccupations'.[17]

Western European states in the 1970s struggled as growth rates stalled everywhere. In Italy, this was a period of political violence known as the '*anni di piombo*' (years of lead). For the celebrated historian of Italy Paul Ginsborg, this was 'an extraordinary period of social ferment' and the 'high season of collective action in the history of the republic'.[18] The end of the post-war consensus in France was announced by the student riots of 1968 and the return of paralysing strikes. In West Germany, the Red Army Faction took on the federal government in a campaign of targeted bombings. They accused the government in Bonn of complicity with the United States' war in Vietnam.

Faced with rising levels of domestic discontent, governments turned away from the EC in favour of national solutions. In 1973, there was a dramatic spike in oil prices, initiated by the Organization of Petroleum Exporting Countries (OPEC), the cartel of oil-producing countries. OPEC was reacting to Western support for Israel in the Yom Kippur War against Arab states. Countries considered too pro-Israeli, like the Dutch, were unable to buy any OPEC-produced oil at all. More Arab-friendly European states like France still had access to Arab oil, though at a higher price. The French foreign minister at the time, Michel Jobert, was so favoured by Arab regimes that he was mockingly known as

'Jobert of Arabia'. The Dutch proposed a pooling of oil sup-
plies in order to help those member states facing embargoes.
This suggestion was met with steely silence.

The causes of the economic crisis were hotly debated.
Businesses criticized the wage settlements pursued by unions, arguing that they served only to stoke inflation and
undermine national competitiveness. Governments worried about rising expectations among their populations.
Economists suggested that Western European economies
needed to adapt themselves to more pedestrian rates of
growth. The period of 'catch-up' – after the long agrarian
depression of 1900–1950 and the destruction of the two
world wars – was over.

The post-war class compromise between business and
labour had given way to a new era of class conflict, but politicians were still hoping to put the post-war settlement back
together again. The commitment to full employment
remained sacrosanct. Trade unions retained their powers
to bargain collectively for higher wages. As growth continued to fall, wages began to outstrip productivity, driving
prices upwards. Governments were unwilling to respond
with higher interest rates because of the effect on employment, preferring a loose monetary policy that kept people in
jobs. Across Western Europe, inflation ballooned, reaching
almost 20 per cent in the UK, almost 25 per cent in Italy
and climbing steadily in many other countries. Only in
West Germany was inflation kept under control (see table
opposite).

National efforts to patch up the post-war compromise
saw governments strike deals with their own workers. In

Table 2.2

Inflation rates in Western Europe (1956–2015)

	1956	1960	1965	1970	1975	1980	1985	1990	1995	2000	2005	2010	2015
France	1.0	4.9	2.3	5.6	14.5	12.9	6.5	3.4	1.7	1.6	1.6	1.1	- 0.4
Germany	1.2	2.3	2.1	3.0	6.5	4.9	2.2	2.7	2.3	1.5	1.4	0.7	- 0.3
Italy	1.8	2.5	5.5	4.3	24.5	20.6	9.4	6.5	3.9	2.2	1.9	1.3	- 0.6
United Kingdom	5.1	- 0.5	4.6	5.0	19.1	18.4	5.4	4.9	2.4	0.8	1.6	3.5	0.3
United States	0.4	1.0	1.0	6.2	12.3	13.9	3.5	5.3	2.8	2.7	3.0	2.6	- 0.1

Source: OECD data (in all years, data are for January)

Britain, this was the era of 'beer and sandwiches' at Downing Street. Trade union representatives, business leaders and government ministers met to hammer out industry-wide pay deals. In France, there was some attempt to shift the burden of adjustment onto workers. Keeping the French franc strong by pegging it to the Deutschmark obliged French industries to cut costs to remain competitive. The strategy didn't last. Leading voices within French industry complained they were being strangled by inflation-obsessed central bankers. The Gaullist Prime Minister Jacques Chirac boosted domestic demand through state spending with the result that France could no longer keep its currency tied to the German mark. It was forced out of the 'snake' in 1976.

A later French effort to adapt to the new era of lower growth was the Barre plan, named after the economics professor Raymond Barre who was made Prime Minister in 1976. This strategy was aimed at keeping wages and prices down and encouraging the kind of structural reforms that Margaret Thatcher made her own after her election in 1979. The Barre plan failed miserably: joblessness in France rose, from 400,000 in 1974 to 1.6 million in 1980; inflation rose from 10 per cent in 1978 to 13.6 per cent in 1980. Violence broke out in one of the country's leading steel-producing regions, the Lorraine. Steelworkers marched to Paris in opposition to the government's policies. In the 1981 presidential elections, the Socialist candidate, François Mitterrand, was swept to power on the back of promises of state-led growth as a way out of France's economic troubles.[19]

Adieu post-war compromise

As all these attempts at preserving the post-war compromise failed, governments eventually began to see things differently. Instead of perceiving it as the route to economic prosperity and social peace, they now saw this compromise as a major obstacle. Governments gave up on the commitment to full employment, raised interest rates to curb inflation and clipped the powers of trade unions. A pioneer of this approach was the US Federal Reserve chairman, Paul Volcker, who launched an era of tight monetary policy in 1979. This dramatically pushed up rates of joblessness in the United States, but brought inflation down from 13.9 per cent in 1980 to 3.5 per cent five years later. Europeans followed suit, peacefully in some cases and more violently in others.

In the UK, Margaret Thatcher took on the trade unions in a bloody struggle between the government and organized labour. The post-war consensus was finally buried when her chancellor, Geoffrey Howe, raised taxes in his 1981 budget, at a time of deep economic recession. In the Netherlands, the country's tradition for consensual politics was the basis for the Wassenaar Accord of 1982, a deal whereby Dutch trade unions accepted wage moderation in the hope it would generate more growth. In 1985, Italians voted in a referendum to reduce the *scala mobile*, a national system introduced after the war to ensure that workers' wages would be protected against inflation. This had some impact on the country's overall economic health, though what really boosted

Italian growth was an end to the bloody violence of the preceding decade.[20]

Where does European integration fit into this dismantling of the post-war compromise? By the mid-1980s, a number of factors came together to bring about a relaunching of European integration. One was the widespread disillusionment with national economic strategies. Governments had tried throughout the 1970s to kick-start their stalling economies on their own, but they had failed. The French experience was emblematic and explains why France played a central role in the new phase of European integration. Mitterrand had been elected in 1981 on the platform of 'Keynesianism in one country' but was unable to boost French growth. With pressure mounting on the French franc, Mitterrand was tempted to take France out of the Exchange Rate Mechanism in a move that would have been a serious blow to plans for European monetary integration. French industry, he thought, would benefit from a cheaper currency. Mitterrand was not convinced, however, that a socialist France could survive if cut off from its European neighbours and he came to believe that national prosperity depended upon the wider European community. His finance minister at the time, Jacques Delors, put it very simply: France, he declared, faces a choice between Europe and decline.

This disillusionment with the government's ability to promote national prosperity was felt especially on the European left. Back in the 1950s and 1960s, socialists had rescued the nation-state in a way that allowed little room for further European integration. The Treaty of Rome had committed its signatories to creating an integrated single market, but social democrats remained attached to state aid and protectionism. As a result, much of the 1957 treaty remained a dead letter. By the mid-1980s, all this had changed. There was an acceptance on the left that growth would come only through the integration of markets. 'Europe' had become a more achievable goal than socialism, and after the bitter struggles of the late 1960s and 1970s it seemed like not such a bad thing to aim for. For those left-wing parties who found themselves out of power, building a 'social Europe' seemed more realistic than trying to stem the tide of neoliberalism at home.

Disillusion with national politics also emanated from Europe's southern periphery. There was a strong conviction in Greece, Spain and Portugal that continued democratization and economic prosperity would only come if these countries were firmly anchored within the European Community. Failed national strategies in Northern Europe coincided with the collapse of political regimes that had structured national life in the South. Together, these developments pushed national elites towards closer European cooperation.

Britain's role in this relaunch of European integration was crucial. Margaret Thatcher pursued a two-step strategy on Europe. She first demanded that the UK be recompensed for its high contributions to the European Community budget. A deal on this was struck at a summit in Fontainebleau, a town 70 kilometres south of Paris, in 1984. Thatcher then turned to her second goal of more market liberalization. Thatcher and Mitterrand worked together on a new deal which became the Single European Act. This was approved by the European Council in December 1985 and entered into force eighteen months later. As well as committing its signatories to realizing the single market by 1992, the Single European Act contained provisions for streamlining decision-making and introducing qualified majority voting in some areas. Countries could still insist on wielding their vetoes on issues of national importance, but the passing of European legislation was made a little easier.

Driving this revival of European integration in the 1980s was a convergence in views among European leaders and governments. They all believed growth would come from closer European cooperation. This had been an alien idea in the Europe of the 1950s and 1960s when politicians across the board had seen national planning and government intervention in the economy as the two pillars of their national growth strategy. The crisis of the 1970s then caused a profound shift in views and an accompanying loss of faith in the power of nation-states to control their own economic fate. Bruised and battered by their efforts to reform their economies at home, governments retreated to the relative safety of European summits, united in their belief that the pursuit of national solutions had proven to be both ineffective and politically damaging. Closer European integration became a way of burying the post-war compromise.

Maastricht and all that

The end of the Cold War came as a great surprise, not least to those most involved in fighting it. Mikhail Gorbachev had come to power with the famous maxim in mind, 'things must change in order to remain the same'. However, by loosening the political control of the centre (*glasnost*) at the same time as introducing some market-based dynamics into Soviet central planning (*perestroika*), he brought down the very system he wanted to save. As the historian Eric Hobsbawm observed, *glasnost* led to a disintegration of political authority and *perestroika* to the destruction of the established mechanisms of economic management. One without the other might have been manageable, as it was in China. Doing both at the same time brought the Soviet Union tumbling down.[21]

For political leaders such as Thatcher and Mitterrand, these were unsettling times. Their initial response was to try to keep the show on the road. They were concerned above all that a reunified Germany would change the balance of power in Europe. Surprisingly, when reunification came, it was without fuss. It made prominent West German intellectuals, like the Nobel Prize-winning author Günter Grass, very nervous and there was some opposition from the Social Democrats. But many Germans greeted it as a natural development. Instead of re-founding the German state on a new basis, with a new constitution, the German Democratic Republic was swallowed up by West Germany.[22] The contrast with the unification of Germany in 1871 is stark. The first unification was long awaited and seen in grandiose terms as the realization of a special German destiny. The reunification in 1990 had something empty and practical about it. It was unexpected and when it came it was overseen with a minimum of fuss, made possible by the largesse of the West German taxpayer. Outside Germany, there was concern about the consequences. Would a reunited Germany seek to impose itself upon the rest of Europe, in particular on

Eastern European states that already had some economic ties with Germany?

Signed in the southern Dutch city of Maastricht by the twelve leaders of France, Germany, Italy, the United Kingdom, Denmark, Spain, Portugal, Greece, Belgium, the Netherlands, Ireland and Luxembourg, the Maastricht Treaty of 1992 can be thought of as an attempt by the French to contain Germany within a more extensive set of rules. The collapse of the Soviet Union occurred sixteen days after the signing of the Treaty and those involved had tried to keep events in the East out of their minds.[23] What they were focused on was the management of a unified Germany. Mitterrand in particular saw the Maastricht Treaty as an opportunity to limit the power of Germany's currency, the Deutschmark, by introducing a single European currency. For a German political elite lacking any appetite for ruling over the rest of Europe, the Treaty was a welcome opportunity to signal to its neighbours that it preferred a 'European Germany' over a 'German Europe'. All sides were agreed that the best model for the European state system was one where individual states were bound together through rules and institutions that no single country could control.

The Maastricht Treaty was not only the work of diplomats. It had deep social roots that reflected the changes in Western Europe between the 1950s and the 1990s.[24] As we have seen, by 1992 governments had given up on their commitment to full employment. They had not, however, dismantled the welfare state. With more people out of work, government spending to support them ballooned. By the end of the 1980s, governments had solved their inflation problem only to replace it with spiralling public debts. In France, the government deficit as a percentage of GDP peaked at 6.3 per cent in 1993, up from 1.9 per cent in 1987.[25] Cutting government spending – or austerity to its critics – became a key political priority and one way of achieving it was European monetary union. Many at the time criticized the convergence criteria outlined in the Maastricht Treaty for being too tough. They consisted of a limit of 2 per cent on annual inflation, a demand that government deficits be below 3 per cent of Gross National Product and that public debt be no greater than 60 per cent of Gross National Product.

For Western European governments, these criteria were an effective way of improving their budgetary positions. Cutting spending and debts in order to remain in Europe's 'top league', as Italian politicians put it, was more popular with citizens than dry arguments about balancing the books. Western Europe's baby boomers had started to accumulate considerable savings and they were less hostile to a regime of monetary tightening than preceding generations. Higher interest rates generated higher returns on their savings. The Maastricht convergence criteria therefore corresponded to the changing structure of wealth accumulation in Western European societies, as well as being a useful tool for governments in their efforts at cutting deficits. Clearly, the EU of today, and the Eurozone's commitment to austerity policies, has its roots in these years. Austerity is not new for the EU, it is part of its post-1990 DNA.

Conclusion

Far from signalling the end of the nation-state, European integration in the 1950s and 1960s helped prop up the Western European state system. The political goals at the time were full employment and rising prosperity, engineered through extensive state involvement in the national economy. At the centre of this 'Golden Age' of growth was a compromise between business and labour, most evident in the building of national welfare states. Europe's population was young, rising wages led to a sense of prosperity, and for the first time a majority on the continent was able to share in the joys of this economic boom. The close connection between the revival of the nation-state and European integration set a natural limit to 'ever closer union'. By the end of the 1960s, the EC existed more in name than in substance.

The 1970s was a decade of change and Western Europe emerged from it a very different place. Politicians had become aware of the limits of national power and neither they nor their citizens really believed that the state was capable of returning Europe to the boom years of the post-war decades. Europe's population was also older and had more to lose. The national welfare state of the post-war era still existed but paying for it had become a systematic problem. The vitality of the nation-state framework had been lost and it was with this sobering realization that European integration was relaunched. As the ambitions of social democrats across Europe had ended in failure and disillusionment, the idea of 'Europe' appeared as a viable alternative and they united with free-market conservatives in the pursuit of growth through the closer integration of markets. Seen in this light, we can better understand why governments today in Europe seek their legitimacy in their relations with each other. The post-war compromise that tied governments to their citizens had been given up, but nothing was put in its place. Governments in Europe have been struggling with the consequences of this ever since.

Is the European Union a Capitalist Club?

Europe's Robin Hood

At the beginning of 2016, the European Commission ordered Belgium to claim back 700 million euros of unpaid corporate taxes. The companies in question are some of Europe's biggest multinationals, such as the Belgian brewer AB InBev, which bottles and sells Budweiser, Leffe and Stella Artois. The Commission's war on corporate tax avoidance has seen high-profile moves against Amazon and its murky tax arrangements in Luxembourg. The Commission has also hit out at Apple's tax record in Ireland. In October 2015, the Commission ordered Luxembourg to recoup tens of millions of euros from the Italian car company Fiat. The Netherlands was told it should claim back similar amounts from the ubiquitous coffee chain Starbucks.

Anger at multinationals fiddling their tax returns has been rampant across Europe ever since austerity policies were introduced by their governments in 2009. 'Tax-shaming' has become a common practice as people react to double standards in tax collection. Grassroots movements, like UK Uncut, have taken on the tax-dodging companies, organizing protests and forcing companies to shut down their stores. As governments turn the screw on citizens in order to balance their own books, why should the biggest and most profitable companies not pay their share? To make this happen, the European Commission has stepped up to the plate. It is a tax collector with a conscience, Europe's Robin Hood.

Or is it? Looking at the moves of the European Commission more closely, the picture gets blurred. Its authority to issue these demands comes from its claim that the various 'sweetheart deals' put together by national governments violate the EU's rules on state aid. In the name of non-discrimination, EU treaties outlaw state aid to specific industries or to individual companies. According to the Commission, attractive tax deals for companies amount to illegal subsidies. Far from welcoming the Commission's moves, governments in the countries affected have responded angrily. The Belgian government said it would appeal against the decision by the Commission. It denied that the tax deals were intended to line the pockets of the top managers of multinational firms. It argued that they are a core part of Belgium's national development plan, as attracting foreign investment is a way to boost growth and provide jobs for citizens. Similar responses have come from governments across the EU.

The Commission presents itself as standing up for citizens of EU member states, but its actions are at odds with the efforts of national governments to set their own employment and growth goals. One might disagree with how they go about it, but the principle that elected governments should be setting goals for their own economy is surely a good one. We see in this example a broader theme: European economic integration advances by scaling back political control over economic life. The ability of national societies to determine where the balance should lie between the public and private sectors has been steadily limited. Instead of seeing this balance as something to be negotiated and fought about in the political arena, European economic integration transforms it into a legal dispute. Only actions compatible with the free movement of goods, services, capital and labour are accepted. Disagreements go to the European Court of Justice and the judges decide. This legalistic process has important redistributive consequences. Returning to the corporate tax evasion example, international investors are in no doubt at all about who benefits most from the rules of the single market. A few days after the European Commission's ruling against AB InBev, a bond issue by the brewer raised a record $46 billion. This was the second biggest corporate issue of its kind ever, and the money is to be used to fund the company's takeover of rival SABMiller, a move that would make it the biggest brewer in the world. If the Commission is a modern-day Robin Hood, then it isn't worrying the big corporations.

This chapter begins by explaining what European economic integration is exactly. It then gives a brief history of this process, from the customs union of 1957 to the single currency of 1999 and beyond. Looking at the effect of European economic integration, we consider how this process has affected our ability as citizens to control the market and to decide for ourselves where the boundary should lie between private pursuits and public obligations. We will see that the EU is not the neoliberal steamroller that its critics on the left make it out to be. The rules of the single market have been in place for a long time, but only after the crisis of post-war capitalism in the 1970s were they used by governments as a way of scaling back their involvement in their own economies. The chapter examines how much integration has occurred in goods, services, labour and capital markets, concluding that no single European economy exists today and nor is there any European economic government in place.

This poses a problem because a powerful political authority is needed if the market is to be controlled or directed in any way. Some hope that the EU will become this authority, but this is more an article of faith than a rational assessment. If we want to give economic life some political direction, then we should turn to our national governments. European states today remain what the French sociologist Patrick Le Galès calls 'policy-making states': huge and powerful political actors whose interventions in society and in the economy still account for almost half of a country's GDP.[1] We must challenge the idea, often suggested by our own politicians, that governments have no power in economic affairs and cannot influence market outcomes.

The stages of economic integration

Perhaps the best definition of economic integration comes from the Hungarian economist and émigré Béla Balassa, who was one of the leading post-war trade economists. Writing in 1961, five years after he fled from Hungary to the United States after the failed 1956 uprising, Balassa outlined the five basic steps of economic integration.[2]

The first is the creation of a free trade area, defined as simply the elimination of tariffs between the members of this area. There are many free trade areas in place today and they have been a common feature of economic history. The United States, Mexico and Canada have a free trade area, known as the North American Free Trade Agreement (NAFTA). Though common, free trade areas can be controversial. The coming into effect of NAFTA in 1994 was the occasion for the beginning of a long uprising by Indians in the Chiapas mountains in Mexico, led by the enigmatic and pipe-smoking hero of the Zapatistas, Subcomandante Marcos. The uprising was provoked by the Mexican government's decision – in order to comply with NAFTA rules – to legalize the privatization and sale of communal Indian land.

The second step was the establishment of a customs union, which requires a single external tariff applied to all member states. There is obviously a significant difference between these two steps. A customs union requires members to give up their ability to set their own external tariffs. Because of the impact on sovereignty, customs unions have been far rarer than free trade areas. Writing in 2011, the Belgian economist André Sapir noted that including the EU there are only eight customs unions formally recognized by the World Trade Organization: the Caribbean Community and Common Market (CARICOM), the Central American Common Market (CACM), Vladimir Putin's Eurasian Economic Community (EAEC),[3] the Southern African Customs Union (SACU) and three bilateral agreements between the EU and Andorra, San Marino and Turkey. Customs unions have generally been an outcome of national integration and state-building. As a country builds up a treasury and a state administration, it also strengthens its borders and unifies the tariffs on goods that cross them. An exception to this was the German *Zollverein*, a customs union that preceded the political unification of Germany.

The third step in Balassa's list is the creation of a common market. He defined this as the elimination of all restrictions on the movements of goods, people, capital and services. The difference between a customs union and a common market is huge. Imagine if NAFTA were transformed into a common market. What would Donald Trump have to say about the free movement of labour between the US and Mexico?

The fourth step is 'economic union'. Balassa defined this as a willingness to harmonize economic policies in order to minimize discrimination caused by member states pursuing policies different from those of their neighbours. There is a clear shift here in the meaning of economic integration. From having been about trade and the elimination of restrictions to movements of people and capital, economic integration in this fourth stage refers to policies. What does this mean in practice? We can imagine a country being willing to support a slightly higher level of inflation than it may wish, in order to keep levels of demand across the economic union high. If one country pursues a policy that helps its economy grow but forces all other members of the economic union into a recession, as Germany did in the early 1990s, then the economic union is not working.

The final stage is 'full economic integration'. This involves transferring monetary and fiscal powers to a supranational authority. Policies used to adjust to economic cycles would also be transferred to this authority. Something like this happened in the United States over the course of the nineteenth century: from being a territory dominated by individual states, the federal level slowly gained in power. By the time a single currency was introduced in 1913, along with the creation of the Federal Reserve System, the individual economies of the fifty states had been merged into one larger economy running from San Francisco in the west through to Washington and Baltimore in the east.

From custom union to single currency

The first stages of European economic integration were dominated by efforts at overcoming the economic logjam produced by the Second World War. Exchange controls were a legacy of the war and they made trade between countries difficult. The European Payments Union (EPU), which ran from 1950 to 1958 and was based on an agreement to gradually remove exchange controls, was a solution to this. The rules of the Payments Union were overseen by the Organization for European Economic Cooperation (OEEC). Described by British foreign minister Ernest Bevin as 'a piece of ad hoc machinery' and run initially by Robert Marjolin, a thirty-seven-year-old Frenchman with an American wife, the OEEC was transformed into the Organization for Economic Cooperation and Development (OECD) and it sits today, comfortably and quite permanently, on the edges of the Bois de Boulogne in Paris.[4] The establishment of a multilateral clearing system with the OEEC did not mean that countries escaped balance of payments crises altogether, however. The

United States devoted $500 million of Marshall Fund aid to help countries faced with such crises.

The European Coal and Steel Community (ECSC) was set up in 1952, soon after the creation of the Payments Union.[5] The same countries that set up the ECSC were behind the Treaty of Rome of 1957, which established a customs union among the six signatory states. This union was formally completed on 1 July 1968, when customs duties between member states were finally removed altogether.[6] This elimination of different customs duties had a significant impact on trade figures. The share of trade between the six EC members rose from 35 per cent to 49 per cent between 1960 and 1970. The absolute volume of trade had also increased dramatically. EC states were trading more in general and more with each other. There is some debate about how much of this increase was due to the EC. Economic growth on its own tends to boost trade: high rates of aggregate demand draw in imports and productivity gains from growth bring down the prices of exports, making them competitive on international markets. Though economists disagree about the exact size of the contribution of the EC, few dispute the idea that the creation of a customs union had a trade-boosting effect for Western Europe.

The elimination of tariffs shifted attention to technical barriers to trade, often known as non-tariff barriers. EC member states had their own approaches to standards and regulation which blocked trade. The 1970s coincided with an economic downturn and support for non-tariff-based protectionist measures increased. After the dramatic rise in intra-EC trade in the 1950s and 1960s, the late 1970s and early

1980s saw a decline in intra-EC imports relative to total imports.

Disputes over trade started to pile up at the European Court of Justice (ECJ).[7] In response, and keen to kick-start European economic integration, the Court made some of its most important judgments. The ECJ attacked national technical barriers to trade in its *Dassonville* ruling of 1974. In the famous *Cassis de Dijon* case of 1979, named after the sweet French liqueur with which one makes *kir*, the Court had to decide whether Germany was right to exclude the French drink on the grounds that its alcohol content was lower than the norm for German liqueurs, with risks to public safety as a result. The Court felt this was not a justified reason and went further in formulating a general principle, namely that products approved to be sold in one country should be considered good enough to be sold in another.[8] Rather than making all standards the same across the European single market, the Court was suggesting that a country needed only to accept that another country's standards were as good as their own. This new principle of 'mutual recognition' became the lynchpin of efforts to complete the single market.

These decisions have gone down in European legal history as turning points in 'ever closer union', but their immediate impact was limited. At the time, many sectors of the economy were closely tied to the state. This included the provision of public services, private monopolies operating under a licence, vast swathes of industry under public control and large public subsidies such as the provision of low-cost housing. Many different fields of social life – from

TV and radio through to education, healthcare, telecommunications and energy – were considered so central to the wider public good that they were outside the remit of competition laws. However, as the German political scientist Fritz Scharpf has argued, this all changed with the rulings of the European Court of Justice. These rulings gave the Court the power to decide where the balance should lie between the activities of the market regulated by competition laws and activities of a more public nature that should be governed differently. Interventions by governments to correct market failures were no longer considered a legitimate form of public action; the four freedoms of the Treaty of Rome had gone from being political goals set by governments to becoming constitutional rules defended by the ECJ.

It took a while for these decisions by the European Court of Justice to be felt. As long as Western European governments were committed to intervention in the economy, then the ECJ's rules were of limited practical effect. However, by the early 1980s, political conditions in member states had changed quite radically and there was much greater willingness to roll back the state and to promote markets in the hope of boosting economic growth. In 1985, encouraged by influential and rather shadowy business lobby groups such as the European Round Table of Industrialists (ERT), Lord Cockfield of Dover (who was Vice-President of the European Commission at the time) produced a White Paper that listed almost 300 obstacles to the completion of the single market – from problems of double taxation to inconsistent rules for the road haulage industry – that were all to be eliminated by 1992. Aware that European leaders such as

Thatcher, Mitterrand and Kohl disagreed on many things, the European Commission President Jacques Delors pushed this Single European Market programme in the hope that all of them could rally around it. They did and the Single European Act entered into law in 1987. It was focused on the institutional changes needed within the EC to facilitate the completion of the single market. The European Commission made full use of the Court's decisions in pursuing its liberalization agenda and governments rarely stood in its way.

The Single Market Programme was accompanied by efforts at harmonizing economic policies. Though some harmonization took place during the 1990s, it was only with the arrival of the single currency in 1999 that significant efforts were made at coordinating the economic policies of member states. Known as the Lisbon Agenda, this document was agreed at a European Council summit in the Portuguese capital in 2000. The agenda set targets for EU member states in areas such as employment rates, spending on research and development, education and training policies, the use of information technology and reform of national social policies.[9] The goal of the Lisbon Strategy was to make Europe, by 2010, 'the most competitive and dynamic knowledge-based economy with sustainable economic growth and greater social cohesion'.

By all accounts, the Lisbon Strategy was a failure. André Sapir's report of 2003 and Wim Kok's report of 2004 both commented on Europe's disappointing growth rates. The European Commission relaunched the Lisbon Agenda in 2005, focusing on raising employment rates and increasing spending on research and development. Five years later, another attempt was made to develop a common economic strategy for Europe: entitled 'Europe 2020', this document set out targets and identified flagship projects to realize them.[10] The Lisbon Agenda and 'Europe 2020' do not involve any shift in economic policy-making to Brussels. Instead, the goal is to bring member states together, to improve the coordination of their respective policies, and to set some goals which they can use when judging their own progress. The European Commission takes its cue from member states.

The most important step, in terms of transfers of authority from national governments to the EU, has been monetary union. The decision to create a common currency was taken at the meeting of heads of state and government in Maastricht and was included in the Maastricht Treaty of 1992. The euro was introduced in 1999 and euro coins and notes replaced centuries-old currencies, such as the French franc and the Dutch guilder, in 2002. The first decade and a half of the twenty-first century was dedicated to managing this new arrangement and adapting to the new monetary powers of the European Central Bank (ECB). It is worth remembering that the Eurozone does not encompass the EU as a whole and a number of countries – nine in total – still set their own interest rates. Two of these, the UK and Sweden, have no desire to join the euro and no one is likely to push them into doing so. The others have promised to join, but at some point in the future, perhaps not for a decade or more.

The legacy of the Eurozone crisis has been to shift some more power to the EU level and to the European Central Bank in particular, but the reality is very messy. The EU's new banking union is built on three pillars: a system of

Eurozone regulatory supervision, common deposit guarantees and a unified policy on managing bank failures. The first pillar has been handed over to the ECB and has meant a considerable expansion in the Bank's powers and responsibilities. The other two pillars are shakier. A plan for a single European deposit guarantee has been shelved as a result of German pressure. In October 2015, Germany made it clear it would not support any such policy and it has asked that reference to the policy be taken out of subsequent European Council conclusions. A common policy on bank failures is in place. The Single Resolution Board was set up at the beginning of 2014, but doubts remain about whether it will be able to do its job.[11] The promise of this Board is that it will shift the cost of bank failures away from taxpayers onto creditors, the so-called bail-in approach. The importance of this is clear. Between 2008 and 2014, Germany set aside 140 billion euros of taxpayers' money to save its banks. The UK devoted roughly the same; Spain well over 80 billion euros; Belgium just over 40 billion euros. By forcing losses onto creditors instead, it is hoped banks will behave less recklessly. The difficulty is that many ordinary citizens invest in various investment products, meaning that under the new rules they would be the ones 'bailed-in', not just the large institutional investors. Pension funds too would take a hit, affecting people's retirement plans. Under the Single Resolution Board's rules, 8 per cent of a bank's liabilities must be lost before taxpayers' money can be used. Many believe the agency will not impose this rule given the political fallout for governments.

Fiscal policy, by contrast, remains the preserve of national governments. Rules are in place for what governments can spend and ignoring these rules means facing the wrath of the European Commission. But more often than not, governments themselves want to meet the fiscal targets set by the Commission. When they don't, they enter into negotiations to get extensions. Italy and France have done this repeatedly. Italy's 2016 budget included plans for a higher-than-expected deficit, partly because of the costs of dealing with the migration crisis and partly because of lower growth, and the Commission has cut Italy some slack. More stringent measures have been introduced since 2008, in response to the Eurozone crisis, which many saw as the result of excessive government spending. But there has been no transfer of fiscal powers to the EU. The idea of a common European treasury was tentatively put forward in a report published in 2015 and signed by the European Union's five presidents. It was ignored by member states. There is no consensus around what fiscal union in Europe would actually look like.[12]

Widen the market and narrow the competition

We know from experience that markets don't usually work the way economists say they do. Free markets are far from being free and what economists call perfect competition (where there are so many sellers in a market that none can influence the price of the good they are selling) exists mainly on paper. The promise of the single market was always that it would improve economic life in Europe by allowing for as efficient an allocation of resources as possible. This boost to efficiency would be felt by consumers through lower prices.

The Scottish philosopher and economist Adam Smith taught us something different. He believed the interests of traders and of manufacturers are 'always in some respects different from, and even opposite to, that of the public. To widen the market and to narrow the competition is always the interest of the dealers.'[13] Opening markets has the effect of securing the interests of powerful producers, the big firms, the big players.

Adam Smith's maxim is perfectly suited to explaining the effects of trade and capital market integration in Europe. Traditional theories of international trade are based on the law of comparative advantage.[14] Economists describe countries in terms of their 'relative factor endowments', meaning the size of their population, how much land a country has and the availability of capital. Given that all countries have different 'endowments', they will be able to produce more cheaply some goods relative to others. If all countries trade freely with one another, then countries will specialize in those goods in which they have a comparative advantage, importing those in which they do not. Trade integration will lead to specialization along these lines and trade will increasingly be between different industries and different goods.

But something else has happened. The creation of the common market has led to a boost in trade of similar goods, what economists call 'intra-industry trade'.[15] Spain has exported cars to Germany and Germany has exported cars back to Spain. Italy has sold coffee machines to Germany and Germany has sold coffee machines back to Italy. The goods sold have become more sophisticated and companies have spent ever-increasing sums on advertising and other ways of gaining an edge in a tough market.

The main reason for this is to do with the kind of markets in which goods are produced and sold. If competition is not perfectly free, and if there is a relatively small number of big producers competing with one another in a tight market, then trade integration will mean an increase in intra-industry trade. Countries in Europe continue to produce many of the same things, and sell them to each other.

This isn't to say that there has been no specialization at all. Eastern European states that entered the single market with an educated workforce and with large amounts of fixed capital have focused their energies on some manufacturing industries. The continued dominance of the City of London, and its role as the centre of euro-denominated trading, is another example. Other forms of national specialization include the construction industry in Spain and Italy, transportation and storage for the Baltic states and communications services in Ireland and Luxembourg. Belgium is big in administrative support services, while textiles, clothing and footwear industries have shifted partly to Europe's southern periphery.[16] But overall this kind of specialization has been limited. More trade in Europe has meant trade in similar goods of an increasing quality and sophistication. This has obviously privileged the biggest firms, who are able to invest in marketing and technology. Industries – from cars through to telecoms – have become dominated by a few giants. They fall short of breaking the EU's anti-monopoly rules, but they dominate the European market and have been able to stifle competition. Whether or not this has been of benefit to consumers is open to debate. Prices are certainly lower in some cases, but market power brings dangers of collusion and price-setting behind the scenes.

The most obvious place where the opening up of markets has led to the dominance of a few big players is in finance. Capital market liberalization was not a goal of the Treaty of Rome. The Treaty stated that the liberalization of capital movements should be limited 'to the extent necessary to ensure the proper functioning of the Common Market'.[17] This wariness came from the fact that governments at that time did not want to relinquish control over interest rates. The interest rate is, after all, just the price of capital. If capital is free to move, then changing its price up or down will simply prompt capital to move, which can be a source of economic instability. Banks are at the heart of capital markets and capital market liberalization has affected the financial sectors in Europe in dramatic ways. The basic function of banks is to channel savings into investments but their role in a capital market is more complicated than that. There are three elements to a capital market: bank credit, debt securities and stock markets. When governments want to raise money, they issue bonds. When traded and exchanged, we call them debt securities. Companies regularly need access to new funds, either to pay for an expansion in their activity or to take over a rival. They can raise money either by borrowing from a bank or by selling off shares in the company, which has the effect of diluting ownership. This latter approach is known as equity financing and stock markets are the place where equities are bought and sold. The bigger and more open a capital market, the more opportunities banks have to make money. The humdrum routine of lending and retail banking – which conjures up the image of the boring but reliable bank manager – is nothing compared to the thrill and excitement of big and deep capital markets. This is where banks connect a global pool of investors with an equally global pool of companies wanting to raise money.

There was very little liberalization of capital accounts between the signing of the Treaty of Rome in 1957 and the mid-1980s. Governments were focused on managing their balance of payments and saw the rate of interest as a key tool at their disposal. In the late 1970s and early 1980s, attitudes began to change, first in the United States and then in Europe. A number of European governments embraced the idea of deregulation. Thatcher's government led the pack, and her 'Big Bang' deregulation of the City of London in 1986 set the pace for others to follow. This wave of deregulation was the result of a breakdown in what had traditionally been a very small network of firms who divided business up between them. British high street banks wanted a piece of the action and supported the government's deregulation drive in order to get it.[18] In France, there was a chronic lack of credit available for domestic business and the government decided it needed to open up its capital market to outsiders.[19] German banks wanted access to higher returns and believed a dynamic German capital market, and the opportunities for fee-based income that it held, was the solution. They realized that German households would never trade the safety of their savings banks for the riskier world of stocks and shares and so they needed access to foreign savers.[20]

The Single Market Programme, launched by Jacques

Delors' Commission, was interested in improving Europe's industrial competitiveness. Big German, French, Italian and British firms were worried about the rise of Japan and the continued challenge from the US. The financial sector and capital markets as a whole were not central to the Delors programme. In spite of this, a Capital Movements Directive was passed in 1988, which abolished limits to capital flows. The Second Banking Coordination Directive of 1989 allowed banks, granted a banking licence in one EU country, to operate in any other EU country. Capital markets were still dominated by national cultures and habits and it was not until the internationalization of European banks in the 1990s that things began to change.

Faced with declining profits on traditional business, Europe's larger banks began to expand into more lucrative areas, investment banking in particular. Deutsche Bank, ABN Amro, BNP Paribas and Société Générale all invested heavily in new activities. The retail activities of banks haven't changed radically and a German, French or British high street will still have the same set of national banks, give or take the odd new arrival or departure (e.g. Santander in the UK, the ubiquity of HSBC in Paris and Amsterdam). These banks have still tended to concentrate their loans in their home markets, even if they have raised their funds from a larger pool. Herein lie some of the problems that broke out in 2008. Banks expanded their capacity for loans by borrowing on newly accessible markets, but relied on a national market for their loan books. This made them very vulnerable to dramatic economic downturns in those national economies in which their loans were concentrated. We saw this in

Ireland and Spain, where many of the funds raised by banks were used to provide loans to builders and buyers in a booming construction industry. When this industry went bust, their balance sheets went from healthy to toxic. Though the economic and financial crisis had very deep roots, many European policy-makers saw it as the result of poor oversight and financial supervision. A European Systemic Risk Board (ESRB) was set up to monitor macro-prudential risks. Existing organizations dating from before the crisis were transformed into independent EU institutions: the European Banking Authority, the European Insurance and Occupational Pension Authority and the European Securities Markets Authority.

The privatization of large banks and their expansion into investment banking has been accompanied by new EU rules to facilitate cross-border activities. The large players have been the primary beneficiaries. However, these changes have come with enormous risks. There are still big differences between national capital markets: bank financing is still central to the way businesses fund their investments in places like Germany or Italy; it is far less important in the UK. Equity markets in Europe remain far smaller than those in the US and many European start-ups have had to look to the US for financing. This uneven integration of capital markets has involved citizens taking on many of the risks, but without experiencing the benefits. The long period of low interest rates that we have seen in Europe is the result of sluggish growth, not efficient capital markets. Most people's main experience of highly integrated capital markets in Europe has come through decisions by their governments to step in to support ailing banks and the costs imposed on them as a result.

Adam Smith is not always right. The opening up of labour markets in Europe has benefited ordinary people willing to take a risk and move to another EU country for work, but it remains a risky business. I moved with my then girlfriend (now wife) from the UK to the Netherlands in 2010 to take up a job at the University of Amsterdam. The experience was remarkably smooth, if you discount a disastrous experience with a removal company whose name we shall not mention. Registering as a resident of the Netherlands, when one has a passport from another EU member state and a job to go to, is easy. It involved a visit to the relevant office in Amsterdam and a short interview with an official. Shortly after that, we were given the all-important *Burgerservicenummer* (a personal public service number).[21] Even swapping my British driving licence for a Dutch one was easy (swapping it back a few years later was not). My wife, also a UK national, settled well and found a job within a couple of months of our arrival in the Netherlands. Language barriers were lifted by Dutch people's remarkable fluency in English. We had friendly neighbours and fell in love with the beauty and charms of Amsterdam. Eighteen months later, for reasons of my work and with a heavy heart, we moved to Paris. Things did not go as smoothly. It was the height of the euro crisis and companies were not hiring. Language was a problem in a way it hadn't been in the Netherlands. Access to the French social security and health system, even for someone with a full-time and permanent job such as myself, proved incredibly difficult. Some of this was to do with the challenges of moving to a global city, one that is wonderful to visit but much harder to live in. There were some great Parisian moments, but on the whole, it was gritty and tough. Another eighteen months later, we moved again, this time back to the UK. The possibilities of intra-EU mobility are there, but moving to work in another EU country is not easy. On my arrival in the UK, I tried to transfer my Dutch and French pension contributions – three years' worth, so quite a bit – into my UK pension. In both cases, I was told that it wouldn't be possible. Had I been ten years older, and had I spent a decade working abroad, this would have been a disaster.

Until the mid-2000s, overall labour mobility in Europe was low. Only just over 1 per cent of total EU citizens lived in an EU member state other than their own.[22] In the US, the rate was about 3 per cent. Migration in Europe since 1945 had been largely in the form of non-EU citizens coming from outside Europe: Turks coming to Germany as guest-workers, Indonesians coming to the Netherlands, Algerians coming to France, Indians, Pakistanis and people born in the Caribbean coming to the UK. The pattern was driven by colonial ties and the demand for labour. Intra-EU mobility was low. The figures today are different. There are approximately 7.3 million EU nationals working in an EU member state that is not their own. Out of a total EU working population of around 242.3 million, that works out at 3 per cent, a number much higher than in 2000. According to the British economist Jonathan Portes, three factors explain this change.[23]

The first is a change in EU law. After the introduction of

the euro, many began to worry that such low levels of intra-EU mobility meant the Eurozone was overly vulnerable to external shocks. Labour mobility is key to determining whether an economy can absorb such a shock. Are people, as Norman Tebbit famously put it in a speech in Blackpool in 1981, willing to 'get on their bikes' and find work? To tackle this problem, the European Commission proposed and member states supported a Free Movement of Citizens Directive in 2004 that made free movement of people within the EU easier. The second factor is enlargement: the entry of eight post-communist states in 2004 and the entry of Bulgaria and Romania in 2007. Many thousands of nationals from these new member states travelled westwards in search of jobs and better lives. The third factor was the economic and financial crisis in Europe that began in 2008, which has added a new dimension to intra-EU migration. In Northern European capitals today, one sees a great many Greeks, Spaniards and Italians, often in their twenties. This is the austerity generation for whom a job at home – where unemployment has reached as high as 50 per cent among young people – has proved almost impossible to find.

Countries have not all been equally affected by these changes. The number of EU nationals from other member states rose to around 5 per cent in the UK, Austria, Belgium, Sweden and Germany, with much of that increase occurring after 2004.[24] It was as high as almost 15 per cent in Ireland, and negligible in Slovakia, Bulgaria and Poland. Countries on the receiving end of intra-EU mobility have complained about the pressure on their social services and the effect on wages of the native population. Sending countries have refused to let their nationals be put into the same box as refugees from Syria and Iraq. In Hungary, the term 'migrant' has many negative connotations and Hungarian Prime Minister Viktor Orbán has asked that Hungarians living in the UK or France be called something different. Some sending countries have warned against the long-term demographic effects of migration: Latvia and Lithuania have both seen their populations fall by 20 per cent between 1990 and 2011, much of that due to emigration.[25]

Why has immigration within the EU become one of the bloc's most controversial topics? The evidence all points in one direction. 'Welfare tourism', meaning migration from one EU country to another simply in order to access welfare payments of the receiving state, is rare. Differences in benefits entitlements are not an important driver of migration, whereas the prospect of finding work is. Intra-EU migrants are more likely to be in employment than natives and given the generally young age of many intra-EU migrants, they tend to lean less heavily on social and health services than the domestic population. Studies point to intra-EU migrants having a positive fiscal effect for the receiving country.[26] It is true that the arrival of large numbers of people can put pressure on services and they need to be able to adapt. Poor planning aggravates problems and if services are short on resources in the first place, then any added pressure on them will be felt more acutely. But the problem here is not migration: it is simply that social services are overstretched. The solution lies in better-funded services, not in closing borders.

The real reason for the controversy is that national

politicians have shied away from discussing immigration. They have treated migration-related conflicts as matters of legal interpretation, passed over to EU lawyers. The best example of this was the British negotiations with the EU on access to in-work benefits for EU migrants. A core part of the British government's renegotiation package, the issue was presented to the European public, and the British public in particular, was one of law, with the actual rights and wrongs of the matter rarely the subject of proper political debate.

Faced with this flight into legal technicalities, insurgent parties have used immigration as a basis for mobilization. Instead of treating intra-EU migration as a legal consequence of the single market, we should return to some basic principles. Societies are constantly changing and change is not always a bad thing. In this case, it is clear that migrants are here to stay. A great many of those who have come from Eastern Europe to places like the UK, Germany or the Netherlands arrived single, but have since married and settled down. In England and Wales, 'more than 6 per cent of all births in England and Wales were to mothers born in the new Member States'.[27] Migrants are putting down roots and should be seen as citizens who are making their lives in the same place as we are. Politicians are unwilling to speak directly about migration because they are afraid of their voters.

An economic constitution

The EU does not have a constitution, or at least nothing that looks like the constitutions that regulate the political systems in countries such as France, Germany or Italy. There was an attempt in the early 2000s to write such a document, but this failed miserably when French and Dutch voters rejected it in 2005. What the EU does have, however, is a sort of economic constitution.[28] In the EU treaties, the rules governing the single market are clear and respect for them is overseen by the European Court of Justice. Past decisions by the ECJ have put it in a position where it decides on the legality of interventions (by national governments or by other actors, public or private) in the economy. The role of a state in an economy was in the past a profoundly political question, debated by parties and shaped by ideological convictions. Today in the EU, this debate has been replaced by a set of rules enshrined in international law that are well outside party politics.

The initiative for this has come from member states, not from the EU itself. It has become increasingly popular over the last couple of decades for national governments to tie their hands in economic policy-making, replacing the discretion of governments with a commitment to follow a rule or by the handing over of policy-making power to an independent actor. Across Europe today, macroeconomic policy-making is dominated by policy rules and independent institutions authorized to act in the interests of national populations. Germany introduced a constitutional debt brake in 2009, which applies to both its federal and state-level governments. In 2011, Germany and France recommended to all other Eurozone member states that they should introduce into their constitutions similar sorts of budget-cutting rules. Many EU member states have fiscal councils, responsible for independently overseeing government tax and spending decisions.[29] Some of these councils, such as the Dutch one, have been around for many years. Others, such as the British Office for Budget Responsibility, the Swedish Fiscal Policy Council and the Slovenian Fiscal Council, are recent creations. Economic policy today is made not by asking what the right thing to do is, but by identifying which rule should be followed.[30] This holds true across all aspects of single-market-related economic integration and also, increasingly, in monetary and fiscal policy.

Shifting economic policy from politics into law is bad for democracy and its effects in Europe have been felt particularly in the area of services. In comparison to trade in goods, trade in services within the EU has increased only slowly. Intra-EU trade in services reached only 5 per cent of GDP in 2007, which is far behind the 17 per cent for intra-EU trade in goods.[31] This difference is striking given how oriented towards the service sector national economies in Europe have become. Services account for around 70 per cent of the EU's GDP and employment, marking a dramatic move away from manufacturing that was the bedrock of economic growth in the nineteenth century and for much of the twentieth century.[32] Some of this increase was due to the expansion of Europe's welfare states after 1945, which led to an explosion in public sector services such as healthcare and childcare. More recently, growth in services has come from the private sector, from finance and media. Though public sector service provision has shrunk in many places, it still accounts for around 40 per cent of service sector employment.[33]

The slow integration in services is easy to understand.[34]

You can buy a coffee machine from a German company and ship it over to your flat in Spain without having to leave the comfort of your sun-warmed balcony. If you want to have your teeth checked by the dentist, however, you will have to get out of the house. You will also have to be able to talk about fillings and sore gums in a foreign language. Builders, plumbers and anyone offering a service have to make sure they are in line with the regulations of the host country and have to be able to ply their trade successfully, usually meaning they have to speak the language. Cross-border trade in services means either opening up a local branch in another country, temporarily moving to another country for a specific job, or having the customer move. None of those things is easy to do.

What makes the role of the ECJ in deciding the rights and wrongs of economic policies problematic in democratic terms is that the issues raised by market integration are usually profoundly political. Trade in services poses big regulatory problems and the principle of mutual recognition is not universally accepted. This is for two reasons. One is that national labour markets have their own standards and there is a fear of a race to the bottom as national systems are opened up to competition – what is known as 'social dumping'. The other reason is that services, public services in particular, are closely tied to people's identities and feelings of belonging. The tradition of public service in France is almost inseparable from the history of the French state and its republican traditions. In the UK, the National Health Service as an institution is at the core of British national identity. Education systems are routinely viewed as part of the wider national psyche, forming as they do shared experiences for the whole population. Labour standards that regulate the service sectors are part of the fabric of a society, particularly for those who fought for them in the first place. To open up these sectors to competition is to fundamentally transform their place and standing in society and any such change should be debated. Within the EU, these issues are recast as matters of law, not of politics.

An example of the controversies raised by services trade came in 2007 in a clash between Laval, a Latvian building company, and the Swedish Builders' Union.[35] The Swedish trade union had sought to apply to the overseas Latvian workers the same labour agreements that exist in the Swedish building industry for Swedish workers. It also tried to negotiate with Laval the wages of these temporary Latvian workers. The negotiations broke down and the Swedish union blockaded Laval's Swedish building sites. The Swedish arm of Laval went into liquidation and the Latvian parent company took the Swedish builders' union to court. This went all the way to the ECJ, and in its decision the Court accepted that when workers are temporarily posted to another EU member state, a minimum level of protection is owed to these workers. However, the Court did not accept that a trade union within the host country could enter into wage negotiations with the company from another EU member state or impose upon it a variety of other labour standards (such as payments to insurance schemes). The Court argued that some kind of floor should exist to prevent the most extreme cases of social dumping.

EU migrants across Europe often face terrible working conditions, where they are paid below the minimum wage, charged high sums for transport to and from work and in some instances are asked to give up their passports by their employers.[36] The Court's decision made clear that this sort of treatment is unacceptable. But foreign companies providing services in another EU state did not have to match the labour standards of the host state. The concern of the Court was to ensure that while a minimum set of labour standards was respected, there were no impediments to competition in the service industries. Far from being objective, the Court was making a decision on an issue that has divided societies and political parties for generations: where the boundary lies between the rights of private companies to make profits and the rights of workers to claim a share of that profit in order to fund improvements in their living standards.

There is today a Services Directive which regulates the trade of services in the EU. It was proposed in 2004 by the Dutch Commissioner Frits Bolkestein in an attempt at liberalizing services that became a key point of debate in the 2005 referendums in France and the Netherlands, particularly in France, where it was seen as opening the door to social dumping. These referendums were not strictly on the question of services, but the French public seized the opportunity of the referendum to say something about the dangers of liberalizing trade in services. The Directive was subject to extensive amendments by the European Parliament, most of them tabled by parliamentarians from Western European states worried about its effects on their domestic service industries. What was passed in 2006 is still in place today: Directive 2006/123 on Services, but it falls short of implementing anything like a single market in services.[37] Political resistance

among the public in Europe has stopped the full implementation of trade in services within the EU's single market, but
in principle there is no reason why the laws of competition
shouldn't apply to the entire service sector, including public
services. Far from resisting this, governments have often
relied on EU law and ECJ decisions as justifications for opening
up their own domestic markets. In those countries where
privatization remains controversial, such as in France, the
opening up of markets has in particular been pursued in
the name of following EU rules. How we run our economies
has become an issue that rests on the interpretation of law
and no longer on the exercise of political judgement.

There is no single European economy and no single European government

One of the ironies of European economic integration is that
while national governments in the EU feel and act as if there
is nothing much they can do to shape the economic direction
of their country, we are as far as we have ever been from
actually having a single European economy. Dramatic changes
have certainly taken place since the late 1940s, and economic
integration in Europe has been considerable, as we have
seen. However, the EU is made up of twenty-eight different
national economies; there is no single European economy
as such.

The reason for this is very simple. With government
spending amounting to between 40 and 50 per cent of GDP,
economies can only be national in form. Government spending, after all, accounts for half of all economic activity.

Looking within countries, these figures are even more striking: in Wales, for instance, government spending accounts for 70 per cent of GDP.[38] A European economy cannot exist when economic life within EU member states remains so heavily influenced and dependent upon spending by national governments.

Patterns of integration have also left national borders firmly in place. Trade integration led to intra-industry specialization rather than one of comparative advantage. Financial market integration has resulted in internationalized banking groups whose loan books are still very national and capital markets have remained heavily shaped by national traditions and practices. Integration in services has been slow and resistance has been fierce given the dangers of seeing labour standards slip in the name of enhancing competition. Intra-EU labour migration has grown, but this is proof of the continued national nature of economic life in Europe: mobility is driven by the differences in Europe's economies, meaning that countries facing severe downturns have become the principal exporters of labour. Where migrants go is determined by the differences in labour markets and the possibility of finding decent paid employment. The starker these differences, the more likely people are to cross borders in search of work.

The introduction of the euro was meant to bring about economic convergence among the members of the Eurozone. The result has been the opposite. We see today more heterogeneity within the Eurozone, not less. Looking at macroeconomic variables, we find systematic differences between Eurozone member states. Looking at the Eurozone's trade figures, we see that four economies – Germany, the Nether-lands, Belgium and Ireland – ran a trade surplus every year from 1999 until the Eurozone crisis blew up in 2008. Portugal, Greece, France and Spain all ran deficits over the same period. Some countries are systematically spending beyond their means, while others are saving and hoarding resources year after year. Private consumption in Germany rose by 2 per cent in 2015, which is the fastest increase in fifteen years.[39] This suggests Germany may be willing to see slightly higher infla-tion at home in the hope that this injects a bit of life into the Eurozone, but the systematic differences between debtors and creditors remains entrenched. We see similar differences when looking at unemployment figures. For the period 2000 to 2015, the differences between member states have been enormous: peaks of 25 per cent unemployment in some countries, lows of less than 5 per cent in others. As the ideas of policy-makers regarding how to run the economy converge, and as our politicians tell us they have less and less room for manoeuvre, given the rules and regulations of the single market and of the euro, real economies in Europe continue to diverge.

We are also as far away as ever from having what the French call a '*gouvernement économique européen*', an economic government for the whole EU. The EU has many common policies but it has not been invested with many dir-ectly redistributive powers. The largest redistributive policy in the EU is the Common Agricultural Policy.[40] In the 1980s, this took up around 70 per cent of the EU's budget; today that figure is closer to 40 per cent. Its goal is to support farmers, of whom there are 13.4 million in the EU. These are often some of the poorest sections of the EU's population. The Common Agricultural Policy has the perverse effect of mainly helping the large landowners. Since 80 per cent of farmland in the EU is owned by only around 20 per cent of farmers, the vast majority of the EU's budget for agriculture ends up in the pocket of the richest farmers, many of them British aristocrats.[41] Those with the smallest landholdings get something like 90 euros a month of EU aid. That might pay for the mobile phone bill of a couple of family members but no more. The CAP also still reflects the original political bargain made when it was set up in the 1950s: of the 43 per cent of EU funds that pay for the CAP, payments to French farmers account for almost half of that total.

Another common EU policy, intended to even out differences between its member states, are the structural and cohesion funds. These funds take up just over 30 per cent of the EU's budget and have played an important role in helping new entrants adjust to life in the EU. The biggest beneficiaries to date are Greece, Spain and Portugal. Between 1985 and 1989, Greece received a whopping 7.9 billion euros from the EC's structural funds.[42] Though significant in some cases, the sums dispensed from the structural and cohesion funds are small in comparison with those spent by national governments on their own populations. New members who joined in 2004 benefited much less from the structural and cohesion funds. Estonians and Hungarians, for instance, received on average 225–30 euros a year per inhabitant for seven years from the EC. Richer countries are net contributors. Each German inhabitant pays roughly between 35 to 50 euros a year; Danes pay each around 125 euros a year. The funds are not distributed in the form of cheques sent to every householder in countries that are net beneficiaries; they are spent mainly on infrastructure projects – upgrading motorways or replacing old bridges with new ones.[43]

Common EU policies do little to affect the balance between rich and poor states in the EU. Growth in new member states has narrowed the gap within the EU, but the real challenge faced by all member states is that of rising inequality at the national level. Data show that over the last few decades, total household disposable income in Europe has grown more slowly than the OECD average.[44] In addition to that, the wealth created has gone overwhelmingly to the richest in society. The trend of a growing gap between rich and poor is most striking in countries like the UK, Germany, Sweden and the Netherlands. Some of this rising inequality comes from the transformation in Europe's welfare states and the enduring differences between national models. For all the economic integration that we have seen, a person's prospects and livelihood in Europe are still determined most of all by local factors: what kind of family they are born into, the skills they possess and the role of their government in redistributing income at the national level. The famous Danish sociologist Gøsta Esping-Andersen wrote about three 'worlds' of welfare provision: the liberal regime (e.g. United Kingdom), the conservative regime (e.g. Germany or Italy) and the social democratic regimes (the Nordic countries), to which we should add today the 'Southern countries' (e.g. Spain, Portugal and Greece).[45] The difference that these models make to a person's life is huge. In a country like Spain, the historically weak role played by the state in

providing welfare has reinforced traditional family struc-
tures. As one Spanish friend pointed out to me, this means
that fewer people are out begging in the street, but it also
means many people are living with their parents well into
their thirties. The French welfare state is impressive, but
much of the burden is placed on employers, so its benefits
are felt most of all by those with proper work contracts. In
Austria, Belgium and Germany, there is a greater reliance
on non-employment-based benefits. Old age pensions are,
however, an important form of state support, and create
significant divisions between the old – who enjoy generous
pensions – and the young, who have no idea what sort
of pensions they may have, if any at all, when they retire.
Overwhelmingly, therefore, your chances in life are shaped
by the country and class you are born into, suggesting that
surprisingly little has changed and that EU member states
are anything but powerless agents, buffeted by the forces of
global competition.

Winds of change have hit Europe's welfare states, evening
out some of these differences but making others more
noticeable. Describing our current economic regime in Europe,
the British sociologist Colin Crouch has called it 'privatized
Keynesianism'.[46] He claims that citizens in the EU still have
the same aspirations as they did in the 'Golden Years' of
post-war European capitalism: they believe in access to
decent housing, education and a life of rewarding work. The
state's ability to deliver this, however, has been replaced by
market provision financed through private forms of credit.
Large government debts are being reduced while individual
private debt levels are rising. In Europe, responsibility for the

risks associated with achieving our life goals is being shifted from the state onto the individual. As a result, new sources of inequality have emerged. Debt-financed consumption has become a reality for poorer sections of the population, while the rich have no need for this. In the UK, it is even possible to get an advance on your student loan – a loan on a loan. In between are Europe's middle classes, whose own version of this new welfare regime involves a growing reliance on rising property prices. Property ownership has become the basis for increases in household wealth and has compensated for stagnant or falling real incomes. Even in European countries that have traditionally had low rates of home ownership, such as Germany and France, urban middle classes are relying on this strategy more and more.

European economic integration has not led to any kind of single 'European social model'. Convergence has been limited as differences between national welfare regimes remain stark. The direction of change has been towards a growing privatization of social provision, made possible by an expansion in private credit. The growing liberalization of Europe's capital markets, pushed by the European Commission, has greased the wheels of this process.

Conclusion

In the post-war period, the imperatives of profit-making were reconciled with the demands of populations keen for a larger slice of the economic cake. Redistributive welfare states were built and national governments became powerful economic agents in their own right, owning and managing industries and banks, and funding a large array of public services. The crisis of this model of 'democratic capitalism' began in the 1970s and many governments in Western Europe have since then tried to extricate themselves from their economic obligations and to dampen the expectations of their citizens. National economic policies were jettisoned as unrealistic and governments of all ideological stripes turned to market liberalization as an alternative.

European economic integration has been at the heart of this transformation. While it helped make the economic boom of the 1950s and 1960s possible, in more recent decades it has played a rather different role. Prior to the changes that began in the 1970s, political and economic imperatives had been of equal importance, with the balance decided by the outcomes of elections and by the fate of parties and political leaders. The most significant contribution of European economic integration has been to upset this balance and to give economic imperatives, in particular the rules of the single market, an elevated status. Decisions by the European Court of Justice have been crucial in this regard, though these decisions alone were not decisive. Only when national governments themselves decided to make use of these decisions did the EU's economic constitution begin to take form. Today, this amounts to an array of rules and institutions devoted to tying the hands of governments in macro-economic policy.

At the heart of European economic integration lies a paradox. We are regularly told that governments are unable to stem the pressures that come with globalization and with membership of the EU's single market and of the Eurozone.

The European Commission and European Court of Justice enforce EU law in a way that gives primacy to the rules of free movement at the expense of any attempts at intervening in market outcomes. And yet, the economic reality is that the EU is still made up of twenty-eight separate and quite different economies. In terms of institutions and policies, the EU lacks any real redistributive powers and it falls far short of being anything like a European economic government. National borders are still decisive in deciding economic outcomes.

We are seeing here the slow uncoupling of capitalism from democracy. The economy increasingly appears as a domain of social life that escapes political, and therefore democratic, control. The lack of political authority at the EU level means that it cannot substitute for the lost powers of national governments. That power has been given up without being transferred elsewhere. Much of economic life in Europe today is left without a political rationale and not subject to scrutiny and debate by domestic publics. Authority is invested in abstract rules and delegated to independent institutions. When European economic integration is discussed, the focus is on the efficient allocation of resources: is capital getting a bit cheaper or not? Are prices falling for consumers in areas like air travel and mobile technology? An equally pressing question is how decisions about our economic life can be reclaimed by citizens in the EU and considered as political choices that we make and justify on their own terms, and not simply in terms of conformity with EU laws and regulations.

Who is Against Europe?

What is Euroscepticism?

Something very curious happens when you criticize the European Union. Rather than being seen as a critic of something the EU does, you are transformed into a strange breed: a 'Eurosceptic'. You are assumed to be critical of the EU as a whole, of its very existence. The term also suggests you are in some way anti-European, a parochial and petty nationalist unable to see further than his roast potatoes, Roquefort cheese, apple strudel or whatever dish is taken as a symbol of a narrow-minded attachment to one's nation-state. For someone who works in the scholarly field known as 'EU studies', the label Eurosceptic is truly toxic. It is like an environmentalist admitting that they have an SUV sitting in their garage.

Why should criticism of one aspect of the EU be transformed into full-blooded opposition to its very existence? We don't do that in national politics. A German sounding off at his own Chancellor will not be called a 'Germano-sceptic'. A Brit unhappy at what goes on inside the Westminster bubble is not accused of wanting to follow Guy Fawkes in blowing up the Palace of Westminster. A Frenchman complaining about the record of his President is not assumed to want an end to the Fifth Republic. Perhaps the only country where this is the case is Israel. Critics of the actions of the Israeli government are regularly accused of anti-Semitism and of wanting to do away with the state of Israel altogether. Why is the label 'Eurosceptic' overwhelmingly used – by the media, academics and in everyday language – to describe those who criticize some aspect of the EU?

According to the Irish political scientist Peter Mair, this happens because political life in Europe has not developed enough.[1] There are no European parties representing different strands of European society. There are no pan-European political debates and no institutions capable of properly hosting them. Unable to express an opposition to a policy or a decision of the EU, critics are forced into the position of being against the Union as a whole.[2] The very idea of 'Euroscepticism' is a lesson in the EU's political under-development. This explanation helps us understand the siege mentality that often takes hold of those operating within the 'Brussels bubble'. Rather than viewing criticism as legitimate, the response is often that the barbarians are at the gate and they must be stopped. Since being appointed President of the European Council in December 2014, Donald Tusk has spoken repeatedly about the danger of the EU being engulfed by populist forces. He has even compared the EU to an apocalyptic fifteenth-century painting by the German Hans Memling, called *The Last Judgement*, implying that a final decision about the EU's fate is imminent.[3]

Mair was right to connect Euroscepticism to the peculiar features of the EU as a political system, one that is unable to organize and to legitimize political opposition to it. But the meaning of Euroscepticism is much broader than that. It has been shaped by the Cold War and its clash of ideologies. More recently, the rise of anti-establishment politics that have gripped Europe has invested it with new meaning. Conventional wisdom has it that for the first three decades of European integration there was a 'permissive consensus' that allowed governments to integrate as much as they wished. This consensus disappeared with Maastricht and since then Euroscepticism has been on the rise. This chapter tells a very different story. The 1950s and 1960s were a time when European integration was contested, especially by those on the left. Analysts think in terms of consensus on Europe in this period because of the higher levels of trust in politicians that prevailed at the time. While in the 1990s Euroscepticism was an eccentric obsession among some conservatives, it has now been absorbed into a deeper hostility to the political class in general, which is redrawing Europe's political map and transforming in radical ways many of its party systems. Its effect on the EU is indirect but potentially devastating.

Who is against Europe?

As long-time supporters of European integration, Italians often thought of membership of the EU as the country's best opportunity to defeat the mafia and modernize impoverished southern Italy. Italians typically trusted the EU much more than their own governments. This is no longer true. In a 2016 newspaper article, Italy's Prime Minister Matteo Renzi declared that 'Europe isn't working for this generation'.[4] Renzi criticized the EU's fixation on reducing budgets, its vacillation in the face of the influx of refugees, its hypocrisy over the building of a common energy policy and its inability to deliver on its promises of investment (there are 'not too many construction sites', he observed caustically). Europe 'has gone missing in action', he wrote. This was not the first time Renzi has criticized the EU. Back in 2014, he compared the European Commission to a 'boring old aunt' lecturing Italy on what reforms it should follow. He also referred to the process of tying the selection of the President of the European Commission to European parliamentary elections as a 'technocratic cut and paste'.[5] Renzi's tirades against the EU have annoyed both Angela Merkel and Jean-Claude Juncker, who have sent not-so-subtle warnings that the negativity has to stop. Renzi's entourage prefers to describe him as 'Eurocritical', not 'Eurosceptic'. However, there are strong domestic reasons for Renzi's decision to turn on the EU. The main opposition in his country is composed of two parties, the Five Star Movement and the Lega Nord (Northern League), who are opposed to Italy's membership of the euro and have denounced the EU as ineffective and staffed by out-of-touch elites. If Italians are losing their faith in Europe, then what must other populations, traditionally more wary of European integration, think?

The EU's saving grace for the moment is that no one has any convincing alternative to it. Faith in national governments is low and a return to the nation-state lacks appeal. International politics is in a mess and hopes of a world government have never appeared more utopian than they do today. This lends to the EU a veneer of vitality. Perhaps one of the greatest ironies of European integration in recent years is that those who are organizing most effectively at the European level are those most hostile to the EU. At the end of January 2016, in a conference centre in Milan, the first convention of the European parliamentary group 'Europe of Nations and Freedom' took place. This group is made up of thirty-eight MEPs: twenty from the National Front in France, five from the Northern League in Italy, four from the Austrian Freedom Party (FPÖ), four from the Dutch Freedom Party (PVV), two from the Polish Congress of the New Right party, one independent MEP from Romania, one MEP from the Flemish nationalist party, the Vlaams Belang, and one disgraced former UK Independence Party (UKIP) MEP, Janice Atkinson, who was expelled from the party in 2015 over an expenses scandal. For now, this remains a fringe group whose weight in Europe is limited. But Marine Le Pen of the French National Front and Matteo Salvini of Lega Nord are rising stars. The Dutch PVV members have as their leader Geert Wilders, an internationally known figure whose party has been active in Dutch politics for a decade. Critical of the EU, these parties above all have national roots and their ambitions are directed at taking power in their national capitals. This may seem to leave the EU unscathed, but this is an illusion. These politicians have an idea of the Europe they would like to see and it is not the EU.

The not-so-permissive consensus

If you read a political science book on the EU, chances are you'll find some reference to the 'permissive consensus' on European integration – the idea that from the 1950s through until the 1970s, European integration was uncontroversial, pursued as an elite project with little sense of going against public wishes.[6] If you read a history book on the same topic, you'll get a very different story. European integration is seen instead as hotly contested throughout much of this period.

The historians are mainly right, but with one important qualification. European integration, even in the early decades, was controversial. Take two of the biggest political forces in the post-war era: the French Communist Party (PCF) and the Italian Communist Party (PCI). They were both opposed to the EC and were able to disseminate their views widely. The PCF articulated its anti-EC views in its newspaper *L'Humanité*, which had a circulation of 110,000–160,000 between the late 1940s and early 1960s.[7] In the 1946 general election in France, the Communists won 25.9 per cent of the vote. Their association with the Resistance made them popular beyond their own immediate constituency of the industrial and urbanized working class. The views of the PCF regarding the EC influenced how French people in general thought about European integration. The French Communists disliked the EC because they associated it with American hegemony and the end of French sovereignty. They called the EC '*L'Europe du capital*' (Europe of capital) and in the late 1970s denounced it as '*L'Europe du chômage*' (Europe of unemployment). For the PCF, the EC was a US-sponsored project that favoured big capitalists, weakened French sovereignty and brought West Germany back in as the key power of Western Europe. The PCF's opposition could be very effective. Communists were instrumental in the rejection of the European Defence Community of 1954, even holding their own versions of local referendums on the issue.[8] They were by no means alone in their suspicion of the EC as an American artefact: many on the Gaullist right believed the same. In France at the time, attitudes to the EC were often shaped by the views held of the US and its role in European affairs.

The Italian Communist Party's attitude to European integration was more nuanced and less hostile. By the mid-1960s, there was a view within the PCI that the EC might be the basis for building a new Europe – as a 'third force' independent from the US and the Soviet Union.[9] Figures such as the PCI leader Enrico Berlinguer, who ran the party in the 1970s and early 1980s, and senior figures in the party such as Giorgio Napolitano – until recently, Italy's President, who played a controversial role in the ousting of Silvio Berlusconi in 2011 – wanted to transform the PCI into a more moderate social democratic party and believed the party should have a more positive view of the EC. However, the PCI remained very critical of European integration. It supported de Gaulle's veto of British membership in 1962 and shared his anti-Americanism. The PCI viewed the EC as an expression of Western power and its influence in those years was huge: its reach extended from Italy's industrial working class into the heart of its middle-class intelligentsia.

In the 1970s, Western European Communist parties revised their attitudes towards the EC. The PCF went from outright opposition to the EC to a strategy of engagement, partly as a result of its failure to convince French voters that the EC was a capitalist plot. French public opinion became more favourable to the EC over time, though one in two French citizens supported de Gaulle throughout his struggle with the EC institutions.[10] The PCF leader in the 1970s, Georges Marchais, captured some of this new-found ambivalence towards the EC when he remarked that 'Europe can be the best and the worst'.

In spite of this rapprochement between the Communists and the EC, the permissive consensus remained elusive. In the UK, the 1975 referendum on membership of the EC was the occasion for virulent debates about the pros and cons of the Common Market. The Conservatives were overwhelmingly in favour, as was a large chunk of the Labour Party. The Labour left, led by Tony Benn, campaigned for exit. Benn was not alone and his opposition to the EC tapped into a long tradition within Labour of scepticism on Europe. When the party's former leader, Hugh Gaitskell, met with one of the EU's founders, Jean Monnet, Gaitskell spent an hour questioning the Frenchman. Writing about this meeting, which he had engineered, the pro-European Roy Jenkins observed anxiously that he had 'never seen less of a meeting of minds'.[11]

Although the EC was the subject of so much disagreement, political scientists are not entirely wrong to describe these decades as a time of permissive consensus on Europe. Disagreement between parties should not be assumed to reflect an equal amount of disagreement among citizens. Western European Communist parties shifted their stance on Europe because public opinion seemed against them. Outside the core vote of the Communist parties, people were more agnostic. The EC was generally associated with growth and access to a better range of consumer products, and while people might not have felt much affection for the EC, they didn't feel a great deal of hostility to it either.

In fact, attitudes to the EC were tied up with much bigger and deeper questions, many of them raised by the Cold War confrontation between East and West. Opponents of the EC were mainly preoccupied with US interference in Europe. They saw the EC as part and parcel of the wider dynamics of Western capitalism and its systematic tendency towards the concentration of capital and the organization of monopolies and trusts. They worried about the EC in a context of nuclear warfare. Disputes about the EC were embedded within ideological disputes and rarely studied simply in terms of the EC itself. People did not consider themselves for or against the EC as such, but rather as defenders of the working class or of free enterprise, as liberals, socialists or communists, as believers in a free market or a centrally planned economy, and as enthusiasts of US leadership in Europe or as opponents of American imperialism.

The 'permissive consensus' refers to a certain attitude which prevailed over the first couple of decades of the post-war period – an attitude of deference and respect for political representatives. This consensus on the EC rested upon a much higher degree of trust in political leaders than exists today. Since much of what counted as European integration was undertaken by political leaders and their teams of civil servants, there was a willingness to let them get on with it. It was this trust which allowed someone like Roy Jenkins to say, when asked why the British had voted in favour of remaining within the EC, that it was because 'they had taken the advice of people they were used to following'.[12] His answer was smug and patrician, but it expressed his confidence that people were willing to toe the political lines laid down for them by their leaders.

This trust rested upon a desire to stay out of politics. Depoliticization and a retreat into the private sphere were significant features of the early post-war decades in Western Europe. In practice, this meant letting the 'professionals' get on with the task of governing. By contrast, whatever a political leader recommends today, people are tempted to do the opposite out of a desire to challenge the establishment.

'A fringe group of tolerated cranks'

Euroscepticism emerged in the early 1990s. The term captures the way a critical attitude towards European integration became a stand-alone political position, sufficient in and of itself and not tied up with wider Cold War questions of geopolitics or capitalism versus socialism. In fact, it is precisely because of the end of the Cold War, and the decline of these ideological debates, that Euroscepticism emerged. As the bigger questions fell to the side, they revealed critics of the EU who were all of a sudden taken seriously as political figures.

In *This Blessed Plot*, the British journalist Hugo Young

gives a description of British Eurosceptics in the years leading up to the Maastricht Treaty of 1992. 'There were always Tory politicians who detested British membership of the European Community from start to finish, top to bottom,' he writes. 'They were part of the scenery, to whom nobody objected because fundamentally they didn't matter. They were admitted, sustained, even promoted, in polite society. But for many years, they also seemed irrelevant, a fringe group of tolerated cranks. What they stood for had, after all, been defeated.'[13]

Young's description is apt as a way of understanding this first emergent phase of Euroscepticism. As a phenomenon, it was politically marginal in all member states and tended to attract eccentrics whose passion for scrutinizing EU legislation was unmatched by anyone around them. Organized around individual personalities, it would be wrong to call it a movement. In the UK, Bill Cash incarnates this era of Euroscepticism perfectly. Identifiable from his height and his pinstriped suits, Cash was also better informed than anyone else about the most arcane aspects of EU treaties. His energy in opposing the EU, from the early 1990s onwards, has been almost unmatched. Cash has long believed that the EU is at its heart an outgrowth of inter-war fascism, a view that was also held by another eccentric Eurosceptic, Sir James Goldsmith. But Cash was unable to translate his personal views about the EU into a wider political movement. Indeed, it is unclear whether this was ever his wish. He preferred to argue the case himself, as a lone figure fighting the federalist tide.

The late Philippe Séguin was the focal point for Eurosceptic sentiment in France in the early 1990s. A prominent figure on the Gaullist right, Séguin led the 'No' campaign during the Maastricht Treaty referendum and was President François Mitterrand's opponent in a famous three-hour televised debate at the Sorbonne in Paris, where a visibly ill Mitterrand battled with Séguin over the general principles and details of the treaty. A more authoritative figure than Bill Cash, Séguin had his own eccentricities: known for smoking almost non-stop his unfiltered Gitanes cigarettes and identifiable from his massive physical presence, his tumbling jowls and the deep bags under his eyes, Séguin was also something of a loner. Achieving neither the presidency nor the job of Prime Minister during his long career in politics, there was something anti-establishment about him that was brought out in the Maastricht campaign. The majority of his own political family on the right was in favour of the Treaty, and he headed a ragtag of opponents. Considering the authority which an ailing François Mitterrand commanded over France's political life, Séguin was an insurgent figure, questioning Europe's impact on French political life. But rather than serving as a launching pad of any sort, Séguin's effort was tied to the referendum campaign itself, leaving no discernible institutional legacy.

The history of opposition to the EU in this period is a history of isolated instances and individuals famous as individuals rather than as carriers of broader social movements. The Danish vote of 2 June 1992, where the Maastricht Treaty was rejected by 50.7 per cent of the votes, with 49.3 per cent voting in favour, was a turning point and had the effect of galvanizing British critics of the Treaty. But the Danes voted again the following year, with 56.7 per cent in favour of ratifying a Treaty to which they had negotiated four opt-outs. Far from being a powerful social force, Euroscepticism was reversible and ephemeral in its effects.

In the Netherlands, Euroscepticism emerged as a coherent phenomenon with the arrival of the populist Pim Fortuyn. His brand of Euroscepticism lacked the obsessiveness and single-mindedness of Cash, and the loftiness and grandeur of Séguin. Instead, it was intertwined with Fortuyn's crass and brash persona and it associated the EU with a political correctness that he abhorred, the kind that spoke of Europe in deferential tones as a 'peace project' and as a promise that the errors of previous generations would never be repeated. Fortuyn lambasted the denigration of national sentiment he associated with Europe and the loss of control over society and politics that came with Dutch involvement in the EU. His criticism of Europe was bound up with his wider critique of the Dutch political elite, whom he accused of autism, of paternalism and of sharing a world-view that had little to do with the ordinary concerns of Dutch citizens. Security, immigration and the failure of the Dutch model of multiculturalism were the issues that loomed largest in Fortuyn's rhetoric, but European integration was present as a factor contributing to an overall loss of control. As the Anglo-Dutch writer Ian Buruma has put it, 'What was it, in a world of multinational business and pan-European bureaucracy, to be Dutch, French or German? People were beginning to feel unrepresented. They no longer knew who was really in charge.'[14] Fortuyn gave political expression to these sentiments and caused an earthquake in Dutch politics.

In the 2002 elections, Fortuyn's party (known as the List Pim Fortuyn) won the second largest number of votes, winning twenty-six seats and coming ahead of established parties such as the Dutch Social Democrats, the PvdA. But Fortuyn himself made a dramatic exit from the political scene shortly before the election: he was shot and killed by an animal rights activist as he left a radio studio in the Amsterdam commuter town of Hilversum.

Euroscepticism was, in this period, an activity of individuals and coteries drawn from the elite, fuelled by fears about national identity. These fears were felt most of all on the right, as the certainties of the Cold War order disappeared. Doubts about the meaning of national identity were projected onto Europe. Someone like Pim Fortuyn was a figure of transition, where the individuated Euroscepticism of Cash or Séguin began to be fused with wider sentiments, all of them convergent in their growing hostility to the political establishment. This shift helps us understand why Euroscepticism has moved from the margins to the centre of national political life in Europe, and why it is now less about the EU as such.

From the margins to the mainstream

On a warm day in early September 2007, an Italian comedian stepped onto a stage and greeted a crowd of over 100,000 people in the Piazza Maggiore in Bologna, a bigger crowd than when Italians had flocked to the square to celebrate their country's success in the World Cup a year before. On the same day, around two million people came together in 220 cities.[15] This was the beginning of the Five Star Movement, founded by Beppe Grillo, a complex figure often described – to English-speaking audiences – as Italy's Michael Moore. The origins of the Five Star Movement lie in Grillo's profound disaffection and disgust for the Italian political establishment, which he calls *'la casta'*.[16] Grillo organized in 2007 a series of simultaneous public demonstrations, under the title of *Vaffanculo* (roughly translated from Italian as 'go fuck yourself'). These were days of rage against the corruption of the political elite and its unexpected success spurred on the building of a country-wide social movement.

The Five Star Movement dates back to Beppe Grillo's blog, which he started writing in 2005.[17] Grillo then began providing 'guarantees' to candidates in local elections, backing them as 'clean' individuals, untainted by ties to the establishment. In 2008 and in 2009, the first local councillors from the Five Star Movement were elected. In 2010, the Movement obtained over half a million votes in regional elections, and in the local elections the next year the Movement put up many more candidates and won almost 10 per cent of the vote in Bologna. The 2012 local elections were a turning point: the Five Star Movement candidates were successful in thirty-four of the seventy-four municipalities in which they had fielded candidates. In the same year, the Movement won the mayoral race in Parma. Citizens of a city saddled with hundreds of millions of euros of debt put their faith in Federico Pizzarotti, an IT consultant with no prior political experience. The electoral earthquake of February 2013, which saw the Five Star Movement crowned as the largest political party in Italy, sparked international interest. The *Grillini*, as members of the Movement are known, descended onto Rome, many of them in their twenties and thirties, with no prior experience of politics. The success of 2013 was repeated the following year in the European elections, where Grillo's Movement came second in the polls. The Five Star Movement is now one of the two main opposition forces in Italy, along with the Northern League. Grillo himself may be tired and some of his supporters are weary of his style of leadership, but as a social and political force the Movement is at the heart of Italian politics and it has brought with it its critique of the EU.

Grillo is critical of the euro in particular and his movement has called for a referendum on euro membership in Italy. He argues that the euro has been created for the benefit of banks rather than of the people. The EU, intended to unite the continent, has divided it and become a nightmare. In his speeches, he returns time and again to the idea of monetary sovereignty: a return of the lira and an Italian central bank that is able to make decisions in the interests of Italians alone. 'We are not at war with ISIS or Russia,' he says. 'We are at war with the European Central Bank.'[18]

Far from being another Cash, Séguin or Fortuyn, Grillo is not defined by his eccentric and personalized criticism of the EU. Rather, he confirms an important shift in the nature of Euroscepticism. His interest in Europe is secondary to many other issues that his movement represents. Grillo's early political career was devoted to exposing, through the medium of comedy, political scandals and corruption. In one memorable scene from the 1980s, he described an imaginary aide asking the Italian socialist Prime Minister, Bettino Craxi, on the occasion of a visit to China, 'if everyone is a socialist here, whom do they steal from?' That joke got Grillo fired from Italian national television, so he turned his attention to investigative journalism, which became the basis for many of his stand-up routines. Two years before the large Italian dairy company Parmalat went bust, Grillo had been commenting to his audiences about the poor state of its finances. Italian judges have regularly consulted him in the course of their own investigations into corruption and malpractice. In the course of the 1980s, Grillo was drawn to environmentalism and this began to shape his political viewpoint. He also befriended Gianroberto Casaleggio, an internet guru who worked with Grillo to set up an online platform for political meetings and voting. Grillo's preference for political activism on the internet is not just because of the more relaxed libel laws. He thinks of it as a space free from politics, capable of generating its own collective intelligence. In his words, the web is the 'medium that gets closest to the truth'.[19] The very meaning of the Five Star Movement itself reflects its practical roots in local politics and local environmental concerns: the five stars represent the movement's five goals of water, environment, transport, connectivity and development.

Grillo's criticisms of the EU and his call for a referendum on the euro have become part of everyday Italian politics. They are not seen as part of his eccentric personality, but rather they belong to the bigger anti-establishment political movement which he founded. In fact, Grillo himself appears rather as an agnostic when it comes to European integration or European democracy. What he believes passionately – as many Italians do – is that it has been usurped by self-serving politicians. The Euroscepticism of the Five Star Movement rests upon a visceral dislike of political elites, which encompasses the EU but is not about Europe in any direct or literal sense. This is almost the opposite of the Euroscepticism of the 1990s, where the object of hatred was the EU alone, balanced against a romantic faith in the integrity and goodwill of national politicians.

This absorption of Euroscepticism into a wider social movement is repeated in a number of other countries. The experience of the UK Independence Party (UKIP) is another case in point. Deep hostility to the EU is, of course, the founding idea of UKIP. When it was first established in 1991 by the London School of Economics professor Alan Sked, it was known as the Anti-Federalist League. Its current leader, Nigel Farage, is often described as a conviction politician and if he has one primary conviction it is probably his antipathy towards Brussels and the EU's institutions. However, this anti-European platform long kept the party in the electoral shadows. For a couple of years, its anti-EU stance was eclipsed by the flamboyant Referendum Party of Sir James Goldsmith, who was able to combine his own desire for a referendum on the EU with an emergent anti-political sentiment that had some appeal to British voters. From the comforts of his house in Belgravia, Goldsmith would declare, sounding rather like a cheeky public schoolboy: 'I vomit on the government.'[20]

Goldsmith's bid for a referendum failed. He remained a figure out of sync with his era, a perma-tanned populist before the age of populist politics. He threw £20 million into his 1997 election campaign and fought in almost every one of the 550 parliamentary seats, but he got only 3.1 per cent of the vote. This was much more than UKIP at the time and not an insignificant share of the vote given the dominance of the two-party system in the UK. But the time was not right: 1997 was the year of Labour's return, headed by a young Tony Blair in whom many millions of people invested their hopes.

Disillusionment came later and it was UKIP that capitalized on it. The New Labour project had created a sense of convergence among the two main parties. Unclear what divided the parties, British society became gripped by a political malaise. This reached a crisis point in 2009 with the parliamentary expenses scandal and the outpouring of anger and disgust that followed it. Up until then, UKIP's performance had been mediocre, but its combination of an anti-EU platform with a more generalized attack on the political class drew many new supporters. The British expenses scandal was in many ways small fry compared with the behaviour of politicians in other European countries: Italian deputies – as Grillo says time and again – have free haircuts, free tennis lessons, are driven around in chauffeured cars and are often embroiled in a legal battle of some kind. But the sight of British MPs engaging in tawdry and tight-fisted schemes to redecorate their houses or pay their daughter's mortgage at the taxpayer's expense was a powerful blow to the image of the British political class.

UKIP added to this explosive mix the issue of immigration. Labour in particular has long treated immigration as a taboo subject, finding itself torn on this issue between the views of a cosmopolitan upper middle-class leadership and a more ambivalent social base. The party was traumatized by a scene in 2010 when Gordon Brown, then Prime Minister and Labour leader, was overheard referring to a Labour supporter as a 'bigot' and was forced – under the glare of the television cameras – to deliver an apology in person. While UKIP may lack a firm footing in the sort of far-right ideology found in France's National Front or Golden Dawn in Greece, its criticism of immigration has a lot to do with tactics and strategy. Nevertheless, it has managed to paint all the mainstream parties as hypocrites and has positioned itself as the party willing to speak 'truthfully' about immigration.

As UKIP's singular focus on the EU has been replaced with a broader programme that mixes together anti-establishment feeling with a social programme appealing to disenchanted working-class voters, its electoral fortunes have changed dramatically.[21] Throughout the 1990s, it contested by-elections with virtually no effect, regularly scoring between 1 per cent and 2 per cent of the votes cast. In the mid to late 2000s, scores improved. Nigel Farage came third in a by-election vote in Bromley and Chislehurst in 2006, scoring 8.1 per cent of the vote. In the Norwich North by-election of 2009, UKIP got 11.8 per cent of the vote. In the last five years, UKIP candidates have regularly scored double figures in by-elections, winning their first MP when Douglas Carswell resigned from the Conservative Party and ran as a UKIP candidate in a November 2014 by-election. Mark Reckless followed him a month later, raising UKIP's count of MPs to two.

Since European elections are run under a proportional representation system, UKIP has traditionally done much better in them. But the general pattern is similar. UKIP came last in the European elections of 1994, with 1 per cent of the vote. It came fourth in 1999 with 7 per cent of the vote, third in 2004 with 16 per cent of the vote, and second in 2009 with 17 per cent of the vote. In 2014 it came top, winning twenty-four seats and getting more than one in four of all the votes cast in the election. In the general election of 2015, it did less well than predicted and its leader, Nigel Farage, failed to win a parliamentary seat. However, UKIP as a whole won over 3.8 million votes, well ahead of the Liberal Democrats (2.4 million) and the Scottish National Party (1.4 million).

Though UKIP received more than double the number of votes of the SNP, they secured one parliamentary seat whereas the SNP got fifty-six. The first-past-the-post electoral system in the UK has worked to keep UKIP well away from government, but the party's 2015 performance suggests it has become an important political and social force in British politics. Europe remains important to its identity, but its success has come after moving away from a relentless focus on the evils of the EU and recasting itself as a right-wing party willing to take a tough stand on issues that the political mainstream is too afraid to address.

Europe's crisis of representation

Hostility towards the EU today is part of a much wider crisis in European politics which does not arise from the EU as such. It is really a crisis of politics *tout court*, driven by hostility to the very political institutions that an earlier generation of Eurosceptics had believed they were defending.

This widely shared scepticism about national politics is transforming party systems beyond recognition in some countries.

In the UK, the seeming 'return to normality' after the May 2015 election was misleading. The number of people who voted for 'challenger parties', like UKIP and the SNP, was staggeringly high. Political change in Britain is pushing with great force against an electoral barrier. Sooner or later, this barrier will break. In Italy, transformations in the party system are equally dramatic. A regional party like the Northern League, and a citizens' movement that has, since its beginnings, refused even to describe itself as a political party, provide the main opposition to a centrist prime minister and his increasingly centrist party. Political spectrums are shifting everywhere. In France, the political right has collapsed into factionalism and is torn between a desire to regain the centre ground and to make a bid for all those millions of far-right National Front votes. Marine Le Pen's long-avowed political goal has been to make her party the number one party of the right in France, and she is getting closer to achieving it by the day. Were she to succeed, this would have huge implications for the French Socialist Party, forcing it to locate itself in the centre as the country's only moderate party of government.[22]

Spain went without a government for months following the elections of December 2015. The rise of two new parties – Podemos and Ciudadanos – has blown apart the traditional two-party model that has prevailed since the beginning of the transition to democracy. The solid fifth of the electorate captured by Podemos is united in its opposition to 'politics as usual'. A new round of elections look likely as each party is afraid of making a deal that may prove electorally fatal in the medium term. Germany, Europe's most powerful country, is ruled by a grand coalition of the two main parties of the right and the left, the CDU and the SPD. As the German sociologist Wolfgang Streeck wrote in 2014, government in Germany is 'firmly in the hands of a centrist national unity party into which the two former *Volkspartieren* (people's parties) have been peacefully dissolved'.[23] A grand coalition such as this gives to German politics an appearance of stability, but it is also a sign that conflicts within society are not being channelled through the political parties, and are instead bubbling away below the surface. In 2010, the word of the year in Germany was *Wutbürger*, meaning 'angry citizen'.[24] Finally, in Greece, W. B. Yeats's famous line, 'Things fall apart; the centre cannot hold', describes very well the tumultuous changes in the country's politics. Since the outbreak of the crisis in 2009, the mainstream parties of the centre-left and the centre-right, PASOK and New Democracy, have imploded. Since the end of January 2015, a new governing alliance has been in power that unites two radical parties: Syriza on the left and Independent Greeks on the right.

The EU survives . . . for now

These changes do not directly challenge the EU, as Europe's crisis of representation is primarily a national one. Often, protesters and critics have little interest in Europe at all. It is their national elites they are angry about. We saw this in many of the anti-austerity protests that broke out across Europe in 2010–12. In some places, such as Greece, there was no way of avoiding the EU, but this was more the exception than the rule. In a 2012 study, conducted by a team from the London School of Economics, it was found that 'Europe' and the European Union were absent from almost all of the protests that shook Europe at the height of the financial crisis.[25] The researchers studied protest movements in the UK, Spain, Germany, Italy and Hungary and concluded that they were all generally national in outlook, driven by anger against politicians, and lacking any direct interest or connection to the EU. An example of this was the Occupy movement's brief spell in the city of Amsterdam.[26] The language of this camp, situated on the Beursplein (Amsterdam's own Wall Street), was Dutch rather than English. Just before its arrival, the neighbouring Dam Square had been the scene of repeated meetings of Spaniards living in Amsterdam who were protesting in solidarity with the *Indignados* movement in Madrid. There was no communication or connection between these two groups. Swept up in a pan-European wave of protests, these actions coexisted in isolation from one another. A common theme might have been the European Union, but it was never invoked.

As Euroscepticism has been absorbed into a wider anti-establishment politics of the twenty-first century, many have taken this as a sign that anti-EU protest is on the wane. At the time of the famous Bolkestein Services Directive discussed in Chapter 3, people mobilized on the streets of Europe. However, soon after the referendums in 2005, much of what had been debated with so much passion was forgotten. European politicians became lulled into a false sense of security. In the 2014 European parliamentary elections, anti-establishment populist parties scored highly in many EU member states. Austria's Freedom Party, France's National Front and the Danish People's Party all scored well over 20 per cent of the vote. Mainstream politicians promised to reform the EU – but nothing was done. Heads of state and government spent their first European Council meeting after the elections squabbling over whether or not to appoint Jean-Claude Juncker as President of the European Commission. 'EU leaders cannot simply ignore the populist howl,' wrote Gideon Rachman of the *Financial Times* on the eve of that European Council summit.[27] They did exactly that.

This complacency comes from the fact that while voters are critical of their own elites, they tend to view the EU fatalistically as the only game in town. Scepticism about national politicians goes hand in hand with scepticism about what politics in general can achieve. Globalization, interdependence, capitalism: these abstract nouns are used to describe the forces that shape our lives. To argue that life would be better without the EU implies a heroic effort of constructing afresh a new model of existence for Europe and for the countries that make it up. In a risk-averse age, replacing the EU with something else is perhaps the riskiest of all projects. In the UK, those arguing for Brexit have no real alternative to propose. There is no new world on offer, no enthusiasm about what might be created in place of EU membership.

In many ways, the EU is like the cartoon character that keeps on running, even when there is no cliff underneath it anymore. As national political systems are transformed by this crisis of representation, social and political movements are emerging that fundamentally challenge some of the basic premises of European integration. As political debate is structured around a conflict between 'us' and 'them', the EU is pulled into the camp of 'them' without having to do anything at all. Its continued momentum derives from the fact that people don't feel there is an obvious alternative to it and anyway they are angrier about their own governments than about the EU. The capacity of national governments to command the will of their citizens is what the EU ultimately rests upon. As anti-establishment feeling becomes a material force in contemporary European politics, so the representative capacities of governments decline. The EU may one day find that the ground it thought it was resting on has simply disappeared, and the EU with it.

Conclusion

Who is against Europe? In the 1950 and 1960s, it was the Communists, along with some on the right whose anti-Americanism shaped their outlook on most political questions. In the 1990s, it was a few political mavericks who were focused on the 'infamies' of the Maastricht Treaty. In the 2000s, trade unions briefly mobilized around the Services Directive and citizens came together to say 'No' to the Constitutional Treaty. By the late 2000s, we witnessed a transition. From being the property of an eccentric elite, Euroscepticism was being absorbed into the wider anti-political mood spreading across Europe. Whereas Eurosceptics in the past had believed fervently in the glory and honour of their national political traditions, today they are more likely to believe that their national political establishments are run by, and for, crooks. The term 'Euroscepticism' – describing a stand-alone ideology based on hostility to the process of European integration – has lost its object. It has become reabsorbed into the changing political currents of the European continent.

The implications for the EU are clear. The EU still functions as a mechanism for the depoliticization of issues, not their repoliticization at the European level, with the result that the EU cannot manage political opposition in the way that national democracies do. To criticize the EU is therefore still perceived as a swipe at the whole European integration project. This explains the long shelf-life for the term Euroscepticism, even when, as a concept, it has ceased to be of much use. With the EU facing unprecedented economic and migratory pressures, the 'for us or against us' mentality of the EU's institutions is stronger than ever before. 'How can you be critical at a time like this?' cry the EU's supporters. Faced with these crises of representation at home, the EU has become a place to hide for embattled political leaders. Viable in the short term, this may prove to be the EU's undoing. After all, the EU is only as strong as its member states. And if they cannot command the authority of their citizens, then the EU is as threatened as they are.

Will the EU Keep on Expanding?

Filling in the holes

I once asked an official within the European Commission whether he thought the EU would keep on expanding. 'Just look at the map,' he answered, pointing his finger at a map of the EU on his office wall. 'We have to fill in all those holes!' Far from having a unified border, the EU is indeed awkwardly stretched across the European continent. Its presence is patchy in Scandinavia, with the whole western flank outside the EU. There is a small but impossible-to-ignore hole at the very heart of Europe, where Switzerland confidently and contentedly sits. There is another, less visible gap further north, where the Russian enclave of Kaliningrad is tucked in between Poland and Lithuania. On the southern shores, there is a big gaping hole where Yugoslavia used to be. That hole is shrinking, but only slowly. The EU's presence in the Baltics is perched precariously between the easterly mass of Russia and Belarus and Ukraine to the south.

A bureaucrat trained to iron out imperfections may wish to tidy up this zigzagging border. Doing so would mean fattening out the eastern border by adding Belarus, Ukraine and

Moldova. A desire for symmetry and order would exclude Turkey, as this would only create a new excrescence into the Asian continent that would require its own set of enlargements. Contributing to a tidier and more contiguous border is not, however, one of the criteria determining entry into the European Union. In principle, the EU is open to any European state that wants to join. Applicant states must commit to respecting and promoting the values listed in article 2 of the EU treaties, such as democracy, human and minority rights, justice and many others.[1]

What article 49 of the EU treaties does not tell us is the criteria we should use when determining whether a country is a European state. Is the criterion a geographical one? If so, then the European continent extends well beyond the Black Sea, encompassing the western territories of Kazakhstan and a good chunk of western Russia. But there could be other criteria as well. What if a state has seceded from an existing European state? Does it still qualify? The EU has so far been very cautious in answering the (as yet hypothetical) calls from Scotland and Catalonia for membership, even if they were to divorce amicably from their existing states. What if we matched EU membership with participation in the Eurovision Song Contest? Contestants for 2016 include Israel and – quite inexplicably – Australia.

Article 49 also limits itself to setting out the conditions determining who is allowed to apply for membership of the EU. It tells us nothing about acceptance or the terms of entry for a new country. This is a matter of negotiation between the EU and the applicant state, which, as we shall see, has not always gone very smoothly. Any decision to accept a new member must have the unanimous support of existing member states and of the European Parliament.

The most successful foreign policy ever?

The EU was awarded the Nobel Peace Prize in 2012 because of 'sixty years of contribution to peace, democracy and the respect for human rights'. As we have already seen, the role of European integration in securing peace in Western Europe after 1945 is dubious. Other factors, most notably the economic boom of the post-war years, played a far greater role. What the Nobel Peace Prize committee was perhaps thinking of was the EU's enlargement policy, celebrated as the 'most successful foreign policy ever' by the *Financial Times* and considered a peaceful version of what US diplomats call 'regime change'.

The idea of enlargement as a tool for promoting democracy usually refers to the EU's role in Eastern Europe. According to former Italian Prime Minister Giuliano Amato, the EU's expansion eastwards was 'nothing short of a political miracle'.[2] The European Commissioner who oversaw the entry into the EU of eight post-communist states in 2004 described it as 'the most epic moment in Europe since 1945'.[3] This view was most popular at the time of the US invasion of Iraq, when an American preference for militarism was contrasted with a more peaceful European approach to the spread of democracy. 'Americans are from Mars,' observed the author Robert Kagan, 'and Europeans are from Venus'.[4]

Attitudes towards EU enlargement have cooled significantly since those heady days of the early 2000s. At the time,

EU enlargement enthusiast Mark Leonard went as far as to suggest that 'Europe can take over the world without becoming a target for hostility'.[5] Far from taking over the world, the EU will struggle to expand further into the Balkans after Croatia's entry in 2013. Conflicts between Serbia and Kosovo remain significant, and many experts are sceptical about the ability of Bosnia-Herzegovina to hold together as a single state. Expansion eastwards is also off the agenda. Concerns about the EU's ability to absorb new members have combined with existential angst about what sort of identity the EU would have if a country like Turkey joined. In the Netherlands, almost half a million people backed an initiative by the GeenPeil (No Poll) campaign group to hold a referendum on the EU's association agreement with Ukraine. With so many feeling that it was an unwelcome step towards eventual Ukrainian membership of the EU, a majority of Dutch voters rejected the association agreement in the referendum.

Doubts about the success of enlargement have also come from the new member states themselves. The events of 1989 are now viewed with some suspicion and historians have been busy rewriting the history of this period. Archives have revealed that decisions made by Mikhail Gorbachev were more important to the fall of the Berlin Wall than previously thought. Was 1989 the result of a collapse of an exhausted elite rather than the overthrow of tyranny by a determined and brave population?[6] Many of Eastern Europe's old dissidents have come to view 1989 as a series of moments staged by the West. According to the late Václav Havel, leading Czech dissident and first president of Czechoslovakia after the end of Communist rule, the term 'Velvet Revolution' was coined by a Western journalist.[7]

Societies across Eastern Europe are struggling with a crisis of expectations. Many have lost faith in the ability of markets and liberal democracy to deliver a better life. In a poll conducted twenty years after the collapse of the Soviet bloc, almost half of all young Hungarians were found to believe that life under 'Goulash communism' – as the Hungarian system was known – was better than life today.[8] This disenchantment extends to life as a member of the EU. Eastern European citizens are the least likely to turn out to vote in European parliamentary elections and the tenth anniversary of EU membership was described by one Hungarian newspaper as an 'invisible birthday'.

European disintegration

This disenchantment with European enlargement has developed hand in hand with something quite new: the possibility that in the future the EU will not grow but shrink. This runs counter to almost every academic theory of European integration and contradicts all those who argue that the EU is designed only to move forward, not backwards. Nevertheless, the terms referring to a shrinking EU have become some of the most popular words used in conversations about the bloc's future. 'Grexit' has become the universal term to describe Greece's exit from the Eurozone. 'Brexit' is used to describe the UK's exit from the EU. Similar terms are beginning to sprout up, often unexpectedly. Marine Le Pen in France has described herself as 'Madame Frexit', saying that were she to become French President she would want a referendum on France's membership of the Eurozone and perhaps even of the EU. 'Dexit' has made an uncertain entry, with some using it to refer to Germany's exit from the Eurozone and others to refer to Denmark's exit from the EU. The most recent addition is 'Nexit': a poll in February 2016 found that 53 per cent of the Dutch wanted their own referendum on EU membership. Were such a vote to be held, Nexit would be a real possibility. The Dutch rejected the Constitutional treaty in 2005 and share many of the criticisms of the EU aired by the British government led by David Cameron.

As ever with something unprecedented, no one really knows what an exit from the EU would look like. According to article 50 of the EU treaties, which sets out the procedure for the exit of a member state from the EU, a head of government needs to make a statement to the rest of the European Council announcing the intention to withdraw. This triggers the beginning of the article 50 process, which involves negotiations on the terms of withdrawal, held between the country that wishes to leave and the rest of the EU.[9] These negotiations will involve twenty-seven member states on one side, and one member state on the other. Existing member states will take their positions and will negotiate as a bloc with the member state who wants to leave. The identity and status of that member state are crucial: a big and powerful member state will be able to extract better terms and drive a harder bargain. But it is still twenty-seven against one. The negotiations themselves must be about the terms of withdrawal and what the new relationship will be between the EU and the now-on-its-way-out member state. They can last for a maximum of two years; any extension after that requires a unanimous vote by existing member states. A popular argument among supporters of Brexit has been that the country should aim for two votes: one for exit, which would send the message to the rest of the EU that the Brits are serious, and a second on the new and improved deal secured with the EU as a result. Article 50 makes it clear that negotiations cannot be about a new deal for the supposedly exiting member state, as that is not what they are for. The article 50 process would be dominated by political calculations and it would be wrong to declare the treaties inviolable. But legally, at least, a second referendum is excluded, as the negotiations between the twenty-seven member states and the country seeking to withdraw would be about exit, not about a new relationship.

European disintegration feels tangible and the sense of inevitability about the expansion of the EU has evaporated in recent years. Nevertheless, the EU's expansion has been one of the most historically significant events in Europe in recent decades. Enlargement has been a deeply political process and has transformed the countries that have applied to join. It may even be that the logic of disintegration seeping into the EU has its roots in the bloc's expansion. One of the great ironies of the EU's enlargement is that while it has overcome some of the divisions of North and South, East and West, the union that has been created is now one of disenchantment. This shared disaffection may be so strong that it tears the EU apart.

A brief history of enlargement

Originally a club of six members (France, Germany, Italy, the Netherlands, Belgium and Luxembourg), there are now twenty-eight members of the EU. The first major expansion was in 1973, when the United Kingdom joined the EC, along with Ireland and Denmark. Norway had also been accepted for membership but its population decided against joining in a referendum in 1972.[10] Ireland and Denmark posed few problems for the existing six members of the EC. Ireland in particular was small and poor, and unlikely to be a drain on the other member states. Denmark was relatively wealthy and would contribute handsomely to the EC's budget.

The UK's story was very different. Entry in 1973 came at the end of a long twelve years of trying to join. An application was first put in by Harold Macmillan's Conservative government in 1962 and was promptly vetoed by General de Gaulle a year later, in a famously lucid and direct televised broadcast. A second application, by Harold Wilson in 1967, was again vetoed by de Gaulle. Negotiations on British membership restarted under Edward Heath and in 1973 the UK entered what was widely known then as the Common Market. Two years later, a referendum was held on a new set of terms for British membership and a majority voted to remain in. It is common to think that the UK's late entry into the EU had been due to a misplaced vision of itself as a global power, what Macmillan called the 'outdated terms of a vanished past'.[11] There is some truth to this. The UK was the dominant state in the international system in the period between the end of the Napoleonic Wars (1815) and the outbreak of the Franco-Prussian War (1870). It was one of a handful of great powers up until 1914 and a key player in brokering the peace settlement of 1918. Adapting to life as a middle-ranking power was never going to be easy.

For all of these delusions of grandeur, the real story of the UK's late entry into the EU is about trade. In 1945, British politicians thought in global terms largely because their trade was global. After decades of European protectionism, the UK's economic ties to continental Europe after the Second World War were weak.[12] Back in 1912, when Britain was still an imperial power, the rest of Europe was its largest export market. Protectionist measures after the First World War put an end to that, as did the UK's own abandonment of free trade in 1932. To compensate for the loss of European markets, British companies focused on the Empire and on Commonwealth countries. By the early 1950s, Australia – with a population far smaller than France's, West Germany's or Italy's – had become the UK's biggest export market.

This was why the UK stayed out of the European Community when it was first formed in the 1950s. If the UK had joined a common market at that time, it would not have been able to maintain the privileged set of tariffs with Commonwealth countries. The UK would have been forced to trade with Australia or India on the same terms as France or Italy did, and this would have hit British exporters terribly hard, given their continued reliance on these markets. In 1956, British troops were sent to Egypt in an effort to retake the Suez Canal, nationalized by the Egyptian leader, Gamal

Abdel Nasser. They were forced to retreat after pressure from the United States, who viewed these imperial gestures as harming the West's fight against the Soviet Union. As documented so well in C. P. Snow's 1964 novel *Corridors of Power*, this debacle led to soul-searching and hand-wringing within the British governing classes. It did not lead directly to the EC, however. What changed between 1952 and 1962 were the UK's trade patterns.

With the disappearance of most of the British Empire, and because of policies pursued by Commonwealth countries that involved raising tariffs on imports in order to encourage domestic industry (so-called import-substitution policies), the importance of trade preferences with colonies and Commonwealth countries declined throughout the 1950s and 1960s. The UK had hoped to exchange some of its special access to these markets for privileged access to the US market. Continued American protectionism, and the introduction of a global tariff reduction regime (the General Agreement on Tariffs and Trade – GATT), put an end to that. Disappointing growth rates raised fears that Britain was falling behind. All these factors resulted in a strategic reorientation by the British government towards the EC.

De Gaulle's opposition to UK entry was implacable, though based on principle more than on any special anti-British sentiment. He also vetoed in 1962 an application from Norway to join the EC. Still smarting from the UK's attempts at torpedoing the EC at its outset and the British move to set up its own trade bloc, known as the European Free Trade Area (EFTA), de Gaulle believed the UK was economically, politically and socially out of touch with the rest of Western

Europe. And he suspected the UK would serve as a Trojan Horse for US interests, making his vision of an independent European power – headed by the French – less likely.

British entry was only possible once de Gaulle had departed from French political life, replaced by a more emollient Georges Pompidou. The warm relationship between Pompidou and Heath did not stop the French from rigging in their favour the financing of the Common Market. The original six members of the EC finalized a deal on financing in 1969 and it was presented to the British on a take-it-or-leave-it basis. Heath took it. This was the 'own resources system', known as such because customs duties raised on goods coming into the Common Market were deemed as belonging to the EC as a whole rather than to the individual member states. What countries put in, based on their own trade patterns, would then be returned to them in the form of subsidies. The British ended up systematically paying in more than they got back. As large importers of food, but with only a small agricultural sector, the UK paid lots of duty on their food imports and got very little back via the Common Agricultural Policy. The French, who imported far less food and had a much larger agricultural sector, were the big winners of this arrangement.[13]

Being a net contributor to the EC budget at a time when it was economically worse off than most other member states was a source of major friction between the UK and the rest of the EC. It was one of the reasons for holding the 1975 referendum on EC membership. Margaret Thatcher and François Mitterrand struggled with one another on this issue in the early 1980s, with Thatcher eventually emerging victorious at the Fontainebleau summit in 1984. Currently, the UK receives back around 66 per cent of what it would otherwise pay into the EU budget, making its net contribution in 2015 around £8.5 billion.[14] This may sound a lot, but budget contributions of member states are a combination of VAT receipts, gross national income, customs duties and levies on sugar production. As the UK is one of the biggest economies in the EU, it will be one of the biggest contributors to the EU budget. The amount also works out at no more than 0.5 per cent of the UK's GDP. As I explained in Chapter 3, the EU does very little by way of redistribution, but it does a bit, which is why big and rich member states like the UK are net contributors.

Coming in from the cold, Mediterranean-style

The next major enlargements were of a quite different kind. They saw the entry of three Southern countries, Portugal, Spain and Greece. Greece joined first, in 1981, and Portugal and Spain joined together in 1986. Membership of the Common Market symbolized an end to the isolation of these countries. Both Spain and Portugal had been ruled by dictators since before Second World War: António de Oliveira Salazar in Portugal took power in 1932, Francisco Franco in Spain in 1939. For decades, these countries had languished as impoverished suburbs to the richer countries in the North. They were known as exporters of cheap labour and as sun-drenched tourist destinations. In the year before Franco's death in 1975, 34 million foreigners visited Spain.[15]

Spain was less economically backward than Portugal and was a member of international bodies such as the World Bank and the International Monetary Fund. It was not a member of the North Atlantic Treaty Organization (Portugal was a founding member of NATO and Greece joined in 1949) and applied unsuccessfully to join the EC in 1962. The cultural revolutions of the 1960s passed both countries by, leaving them with an antiquated, almost nineteenth-century feel that has been depicted so cleverly by Pedro Almodóvar in his films. In Greece's case, military rule only lasted seven years, between 1967 and 1974. The colonels running the country were an anti-modern and parochial lot. As well as brutally clamping down on the political left, they wanted to make Greece economically self-reliant and they banned long hair, pop music and mini-skirts.[16]

Powerful political and economic forces were at work in this enlargement round. Politically, the entry of Portugal, Spain and Greece into the EC coincided with a tense period in the Cold War. In all cases, there was a concern that further isolation would push these countries onto the path of political radicalism. In Portugal, the military revolt against Marcello Caetano (Salazar's chosen successor) opened up Portuguese politics for the first time in generations. Instability and uncertainty followed, with outside observers fearing a takeover from the far left. In Spain, the struggle between the Communists and Socialists was a concern for European leaders such as West Germany's Willy Brandt. Keen to ensure that political moderation would prevail, EC membership was used as a tool of political de-radicalization.

The international security situation was another concern. The US and the existing members of the EC wanted to keep Portugal and Greece in NATO and to encourage Spain to join. Left-wing parties in these countries – such as the Socialist Party (PSOE) in Spain – had long been opponents of NATO. By offering EC membership, it was hoped this would weaken left-wing opposition to NATO. It worked in Spain, where the Socialist leader Felipe González won over his party's supporters to NATO, craftily bundling it together with EC membership. A referendum on Spain's adhesion to NATO was held in 1986 – timed to coincide with Spanish entry into the EC – with González a vocal defender of membership.[17]

The accession of three relatively poor and agrarian countries to the EC posed a number of problems. Greece was small enough for its application not to trouble any of the other member states too much, though there was some concern at its readiness to join the EC. As the table opposite shows, Greece's entry into the EC had some effect on the area's total population, but almost no effect on its GDP. Spain posed a problem for France as it produced a number of goods that the French also produced but at a lower cost. These were also poor countries with large populations and thus likely to soak up many of the EC's funds earmarked for redistribution from rich to poor member states. Agreements were eventually found that kept all member states happy. France insisted on long transitional periods before Spain could have equal access to the Common Market. Negotiations on Spanish and Portuguese membership lasted nine long years.

For Portugal, Greece and Spain, membership of the EC

		IMPORTANCE OF THE AREA	
	NUMBER OF COUNTRIES	POPULATION (MILLIONS)	SHARE OF EUROPE'S TOTAL GDP (%)
1957 Treaty of Rome	6	167	49
1973 UK, Ireland and Denmark join	9	257	68
1981 Greek membership	10	271	69
1986 Entry of Spain and Portugal	12	322	77
1990 German reunification	12	346	82
1995 Sweden, Finland and Austria join	15	373	88
2004 8 post-Soviet states join plus Cyprus and Malta	25	456	95
2007 Bulgaria and Romania join	27	489	96

Table 5.1

Enlargement's impact on the EC/EU

Source: Eichengreen and Boltho, 2010[18]

was tied up with their fundamental transformation as states and as societies. For many Portuguese, Greeks and Spaniards, EC membership pointed towards a loosening of their national identities and the building of a more secular, consumer-oriented society. At the same time, it coincided with another, more conservative instinct, namely a deep desire among Greeks and citizens of the Iberian Peninsula to lead a 'normal' life, free from the stifling conservatism of the past and from the intimidating promises of radical change made by the far left. Political experimentation was over and people craved stability.

The consequences of this broader transformation have been to make any sort of national existence separate from the EU difficult to conceive. This is why Greece in recent times has found it so difficult even to contemplate the possibility of exiting the EU. To do so would be to undermine the very foundations of the Greek state, based as they are on this return to Europe as a measure of the country's modernity. Greek support for the EU has ended up being a version of the idea that 'there is no alternative': grudging acceptance of a situation that no one really likes but feels powerless to change.

A dramatic example of this transformation of Iberian nation-states into EU member states was seen recently in Portugal. In a general election held on 4 October 2015, the centre-right coalition led by Pedro Passos Coelho had emerged as the largest force, but without an outright majority in Parliament. Three other parties in the Portuguese parliament, the Socialists, Communists and the Left Alliance, signalled a willingness to form a government of their own that would have commanded a majority. However, the President, whose responsibility it is to oversee the formation of a new government, declared live on Portuguese television that he would not give this left-wing bloc a chance, because both the Communists and the Left Alliance were critical of Portugal's membership of the EU, of the Eurozone and of NATO. Such criticism, argued Aníbal Cavaco Silva, is a violation of Portugal's constitution.[19]

In fact, there is nothing in the country's constitution that commits it to membership of the EU and NATO. Cavaco Silva suggested that national democracy in Portugal relies for its survival on the country's membership of these organizations rather than simply on the will of the Portuguese people. A fair reflection of how the Portuguese state and political system has evolved since 1974, it presents the consequences of EU enlargement in a much darker light. In the end, Cavaco Silva was defeated as the right-wing minority government he had appointed lasted only a couple of weeks and was replaced by the left-wing alliance that the President had warned was unconstitutional. Cavaco Silva may have had the last word, however. The Socialist Prime Minister António Costa promised that his government would be fully committed to both euro membership and the EU's fiscal compact that places clear limits on government spending for Eurozone members.[20]

The next round of enlargement took place in the mid-1990s. Known misleadingly as the 'Nordic enlargement', it saw the entry of Sweden, Austria and Finland into the EU. The context for this enlargement was the end of the Cold War and its impact on the neutrality policies of these countries.

When Western Europe was firmly within the US camp in the fight against the Soviet Union, neutrality prevented these countries from joining the EC. With the end of the Cold War, this barrier disappeared. As these were relatively rich countries that would not be a drain on the EU's resources, their membership posed no great problems. All three countries joined in 1995, swiftly and with little fanfare.

The big bang: East joins West

Something has ended
nothing wants to begin
Perhaps it has already begun

TADEUSZ RÓŻEWICZ, 'A DIDACTIC STORY'[21]

The biggest round of enlargement so far has come to be known as the 'big bang': the entry of ten new member states in 2004, eight of which were countries that had been part of the Soviet bloc. This section focuses on the 2004 enlargement, though many of the issues raised apply just as well to the 'mini-bang' of 2007, when Romania and Bulgaria joined the EU, and the most recent addition of Croatia in 2013.

The 2004 enlargement has been the most debated and the most controversial. The process itself was very different from previous enlargements: it was longer, more intrusive and more transformational for the applicant states. Even though these countries joined in 2004, the process continues. All countries are formally required to adopt the euro and so far Cyprus, Malta, the Baltic States, Slovenia and Slovakia have done so.[22]

There was nothing inevitable about this Eastern enlargement. France feared that it would seriously dilute the existing EC and worried in particular that such a large increase in membership would hinder her capacity to lead the EU.[23] France was also aware that many of these countries felt stronger ties to Germany than to France itself and that their membership risked creating a German-led bloc within the EU. For this very reason, the British were strongly in favour of Eastern enlargement. They believed that it would reinforce their own vision of a market-based EC with little pretension to becoming an integrated political union. Both the UK and France were concerned that if Central and Eastern European states remained outside the EU, German influence over them would be even stronger. A German-led bloc within the EU was probably better than one outside it.

All of these different considerations led to hesitation and uncertainty. The messages sent to Eastern Europe were mixed: warm words assuring them of their place as European states, but cooler statements on enlargement as a 'long-term perspective'. There was also much disagreement about who should join and when. The Swedes pushed for the inclusion of Estonia, Germany wanted to fast-track Poland, Hungary and the Czech Republic, and France insisted on its close ally in the region, Romania.[24] In the end, the aggregation of these different positions culminated in the final 'big bang' effect.

Agreement came in 1999, at the EU's Helsinki Summit where EU leaders committed themselves to accepting up to twelve new member states (and thirteen if we include the vaguer promises made to Turkey). The timing had to do with the internal preoccupations of the EU. Its members were split over NATO's intervention in Kosovo, the European Parliament had dismissed the whole European Commission under charges of corruption, and the completion of European Monetary Union had left a hole at the heart of EU integration.[25] It was also becoming almost impossible to reconcile the idea of the EU as an open community of democratic states with the exclusion of all of Central and Eastern Europe's new democracies.

The process of joining was more complex for Eastern Europe than for any of the earlier applicant countries. It was longer, more technical and more intrusive than before. It was organized around the ideas of conditionality and compliance rather than simply through negotiations between governments. One reason was that the EU itself had changed. It was no longer just a common market, but included a common currency and shared policy-making in many new areas. Conditionality refers to the idea that a country must show that it has met certain conditions in order for it to be accepted as a new member. In 1993, European leaders came up with the Copenhagen criteria. These criteria were aimed at making sure Eastern European applicants had achieved their transition to liberal market democracies before they were admitted into the EU. They specified that a country had to have institutions capable of supporting a democratic political system and a functioning market economy able to handle the competitive effects of entering the EU's common market. The criteria also required that a country be able and willing to take on all of the obligations of membership, including that of joining the single currency. The main purpose of these criteria was to exclude as few applicants as possible while giving existing EU member states full discretion in deciding who joins and who doesn't. A more rigid framework based on the need for applicant states to adopt all of the EU's laws was added in the late 1990s. These laws were grouped into over thirty separate 'chapters', each of which was dealt with separately by dedicated teams of experts and negotiators. To 'close' these chapters, applicant states had to pass an enormous amount of legislation and convince officials within the European Commission that the necessary reforms had been put in place.

This process profoundly changed the economies, political systems and societies of the candidate countries. Any disagreements between existing national policies and the EU were resolved in favour of the EU. Government policies aimed at supporting local industries, for instance, violated EU rules against state aid. Eliminating these policies had a dramatic effect on government spending priorities. In Bulgaria, the elimination of subsidies to industry resulted in a fall of over 35 per cent in the government's total budget expenditure.[26] Policies supporting the agricultural sector met the same fate. Poland, whose government was attempting to modernize its rural economy (Poland at the time of joining the EU had 2 million farmers; the EU as a whole had 7 million), found that direct payments to farmers were illegal under EU law. Environmental regulations developed by the post-industrial societies of Western Europe had to be taken on by the still heavily industrialized societies of Eastern Europe, resulting in disagreements unresolved even to this day. In implementing this enormous legislative blueprint, candidate states had little room to adapt laws to local needs and circumstances.

To manage this process, applicant states built dedicated teams of experts, clustered in so-called 'European offices'. This often drew on the most talented members of the country's bureaucracy – those with ambition and the requisite language skills. Islands of expertise were created within national bureaucracies and were usually controlled directly by the Prime Minister's or President's office. The enlargement process strengthened the executive by making it the privileged interlocutor with the EU. The consequence for parliaments in applicant states was dramatic. After the fall of the Iron Curtain, parliaments in Eastern Europe had been viewed as the most legitimate branch of government; they were the real representatives of the people in a new age of democratic government. Enlargement changed that. 'Governing parliaments', as the Hungarian political scientist Attila Ágh called them, were replaced by bodies whose role was to rubber-stamp EU legislation.[27]

Citizens of applicant states were aware of these developments. They saw the proliferation of new laws and viewed many of them with scepticism. In some places, EU-inspired regulations were seen as similar to those which had come from Moscow in Soviet times. In Estonia, people reinvented the old habit of 'double-think' that dated back to when the country was part of the USSR – doing one thing, but thinking something quite different.[28] In many candidate states, it was common for new laws not to be implemented. As one group of analysts put it, non-fulfilment is a 'strategy of resistance as well as a sign of alienation'.[29]

Over time, given how many issues were covered by EU enlargement, a feeling grew of being able to change governments but not to change policies.[30] Enlargement was increasingly seen as an inevitability rather than a choice made by citizens. Only in Slovenia and Lithuania did a majority of the population turn out to vote in the referendum on EU membership; elsewhere turn-out was low.[31]

Defenders of the EU's enlargement process would say that this was all necessary to ensure that a country was in good enough shape to manage the pressures and demands of being a member of the EU. Once a member, conditionality would end and new entrants would play a full and equal role in European integration. In fact, after 2004, the enlargement process did not come to an end – a distinctive feature of the 'big bang' enlargement is that it has continued well beyond 2004.

Joining the Eurozone

The continuation stems from an obligation on the part of new member states to adopt the euro. The UK and Denmark have opt-outs on this, which became part of the Maastricht Treaty. Sweden has no opt-out but it remains outside the Eurozone. In theory, it should join once it has made the necessary changes to its domestic laws, but in practice it prefers to keep the euro at arm's length. Countries that joined the EU in 2004 were not offered any opt-out; the Eurozone was the required destination. After the economic and financial crisis in Europe, and the continuing problems of the Eurozone, there is increasing wariness about giving up national currencies for the euro. In Poland, people speak of a decade before the zloty is replaced with the euro. But legally speaking, the obligation is there and the question is not if but when.

Joining the Eurozone is almost as complicated as joining the EU itself. There is very little applicants can do to influence the conditions which they have to meet. The Eastern European states that joined in 2004, along with Cyprus and Malta, represent 35 per cent of the Eurozone's population but only 7 per cent of its GDP. They are policy-takers, not policy-makers. The formal criteria for Eurozone membership are set out in the table opposite.

Alongside these formal criteria, there are a number of others that are less visible but just as important. One requirement is that a country's national central bank be independent from any political influence. Applicant countries must also be able to show that they have on their statute books provisions about prohibiting any direct central bank financing of the public sector. For a country where raising money on international debt markets is not easy, these conditions affect greatly how much money governments can spend on domestic policies. Adopting the euro also means participating in surveillance procedures that require regular visits of EU officials. There is a pre-accession fiscal surveillance procedure intended to vet a country's tax-raising capacities. The EU's statistical agency, Eurostat, checks that national accounts are properly calculated and published. The European Central Bank is involved in regular monitoring and benchmarking exercises. The European Commission writes 'convergence reports' on the progress – or lack

INFLATION

Not more than 1.5% above the average of the three best-performing member states

---

INTEREST RATES

Not more than 2% above the average of the three best-performing member states selected for the inflation criterion

---

EXCHANGE RATES

Participation in ERM II for at least two years, without major problems

---

GOVERNMENT DEFICITS

No more than 3% of GDP

GOVERNMENT DEBT

No more than 60% of GDP

Table 5.2

Convergence criteria for Eurozone membership

Source: European Commission

of progress – by applicant states. Officials from the ECB, Eurostat and Eurozone member states are sent to applicant states to provide advice and expertise, a process known as 'twinning'.

Beyond all of these administrative checks, it is also crucial that applicants share the worldview about how to run the economy that underpins the working of the Eurozone. The implication of central bank independence and the various fiscal and monetary criteria is that good macroeconomic policy is defined by sound money and balanced public finances. Applying to adopt the euro means that any sort of fundamental debate about what macroeconomic policy a government should adopt is out of the question. Eurozone accession is one of the reasons for the ideological convergence that occurred across Eastern Europe during much of the early 2000s.

As with EU membership itself, the process of joining the Eurozone is reshaping Eastern European states, institutionally and politically. It has concentrated a lot of power in the national central bank, which is responsible for much of the interaction with the Eurozone institutions. Central bankers and central bank officials have come to exercise a huge amount of power, often at the expense of political representatives.

Political debates about macroeconomic policy have become restricted to a very narrow and technical set of issues. Parties struggle to compete against one another when the issues over which they can disagree are so limited Political competition, particularly around economic issues, is sucked out of countries seeking to adopt the euro. Indeed, the implication of the convergence criteria themselves is that the key goals of macroeconomic policy should no longer be subject to political contestation. They should be depoliticized and given over to central bank officials.

Stuck in transition

The political effects of enlargement are clearly mixed. Stabilization after the transition to democracy has combined with a narrowing of political possibilities. What of the economic impact of enlargement? Many have suggested that EU enlargement has brought prosperity and wealth to the former Soviet bloc and the results of the economic transition in Eastern Europe are positive in many respects. Countries in this region have consistently outperformed the euro area as a whole. Average real GDP growth in ten Central and Eastern European states was almost 6 per cent over the 2004–8 period. In the same period, the average growth rate of twelve members of the euro area was only 2.5 per cent. Post-2008 GDP growth in Eastern Europe has fallen to around 2.5 per cent, but even that is higher than the anaemic 0.5 per cent posted by euro area countries. Convergence towards EU averages has also been impressive. GDP per capita in Eastern European countries was around 50 per cent of euro area countries in 2004. By 2008, that had risen to 58 per cent and by 2014 it had risen to 64 per cent. In some reports, it was found that GDP per capita in some Eastern European states had overtaken that of existing EU member states. In 2012, the Czech Republic overtook Portugal and some Eastern European cities boast higher GDP per capita rates than Vienna.

But statistics can be misleading. Convergence rates across

SHOCK THERAPY AND ITS AFTER-EFFECTS (1989–95)

Poland was the home of 'shock therapy', embodied in the radical Balcerowicz Plan adopted in 1989. Dramatic economic reforms were initiated in Bulgaria in February 1991. Czech economic reform was led by zealous reformer Vaclav Klaus. Romania, in contrast, pursued a 'therapy, not shock' approach to transition.

EMERGING MARKET CRISES (1995–2000)

In Bulgaria, inflation reached 311 per cent in 1996; rates of interest were raised to above 300 per cent in the same year. GDP in Bulgaria fell 11 per cent in 1996 and 13 per cent in the first two months of 1997. A currency board was introduced in 1997 with the Bulgarian lev tied to the German mark, then after 1999 to the euro. A currency crisis in the Czech Republic in 1997 forced the government to abandon its fixed exchange rate. The Czech current account deficit in 1996 was 9.2 per cent of GDP, higher than in Thailand and Malaysia, two countries that experienced severe crises in this period. In March 1995, a stabilization programme known as the 'Bokros package' was intro-duced in Hungary, with the goal of reducing the country's high current account and fiscal deficits. It involved a 9 per cent devaluation of the forint, wage and consumption cuts, and a restructuring of the public sector. The Romanian economy overheated in 1997 and inflation rates exploded. It suffered a major recession in 1997–8.

BOOM (2000–2008)

The global economic boom at the beginning of the 21st century saw a large increase in capital flows to Eastern European countries, enabling them to finance current account deficits. Post-2004, access to credit for private households was much improved, resulting in a consumption boom. Northern European banks targeted Eastern Europe as profit margins were higher due to higher interest rates.

BUST (2008–16)

Eastern Europe was hard hit by the 2008 crisis, in particular because of its reliance upon foreign capital during the boom period. Economies across the region went into recession and saw a 6 per cent fall in GDP in 2009. Some recovered quickly but many have struggled. Hungary, the Czech Republic and Slovenia experienced another recession in 2012. In Slovenia, the cumulative decline in GDP since 2008 reached 11 per cent by the end of 2013, a figure second only to Greece's dramatic 23 per cent decline. Slovenia only narrowly avoided an EU/ IMF bail-out when its three main state-controlled banks collapsed in 2013.

Table 5.3

Post-1989 economic transition

Source: Feldman 2006; Bönker 2006; Greskovits 2006; Horvath 1999; Economist 2013[32]

Eastern Europe as a whole mask important differences between countries. Generally, the richer the country is, the less improvement it has seen. Slovenia, for instance, has seen no real convergence with Western Europe over the last decade. Hungary and the Czech Republic have seen very little, with the greatest catching-up taking place in the Baltic States, Poland, Romania and Slovakia. The quality of growth has also varied. High growth rates have been driven in some places by a credit boom, encouraged by private lending coming from foreign (often Austrian) banks.[33] In the Czech Republic in 2003, foreign banks owned 96 per cent of the country's total banking assets; in Estonia, the figure was 97.5 per cent and in Slovakia it was 96.3 per cent.[34] In other places, growth has been export-led and therefore more sustainable. Per capita convergence figures mask great disparities within countries. The wealth of Eastern European capitals rarely extends much outside of the cities' boundaries. Even within the cities, per capita GDP figures tend to measure concentrations of corporate wealth as well as just household wealth.

Taking the 1989–2015 period as a whole, the economic experience of Eastern European countries falls into four periods (see Table 5.3). These periods do not match up perfectly with the experience of every post-communist state that has joined the EU in 2004, but there is a broad correspondence.

Viewing Eastern Europe's transition to capitalism solely through the lens of EU enlargement is misleading. The experiences of these countries are closest to those of emerging economies in general. The 'big bang' enlargement was important as a one-off boost to growth in these countries, particularly by providing access to the single market and by stabilizing the expectations of foreign investors. However, in spite of EU membership, these countries are still seeking, often unsuccessfully, sustainable forms of growth that are independent of the economic fortunes of the richer economies. The boom-bust experience of the twenty-first century suggests this independence has not yet been found. Cross-border lending was crucial to the credit-fuelled boom of the 2000s, but it was the easy availability of credit that also dragged countries like Slovenia to the verge of financial ruin.

Eastern European economies face specific challenges. An ageing and declining population combined with high levels of emigration will shrink the labour market further. Savings rates are very low and in the absence of more foreign investment, investment rates will fall below what is necessary for these countries to achieve high growth rates in the medium to long term. The low-hanging fruit of the early transition era, along with the one-off gains from EU membership, have gone. Government policies will matter more than ever before in determining whether these countries will continue to converge with Western Europe or whether they will remain, in the words of a report by the European Bank for Reconstruction and Development, 'stuck in transition'.[35]

Conclusion: Europe's union of disenchantment

In October 2015, the right-wing Law and Justice Party won Poland's general elections. Within a few weeks, the new government had begun to target the country's constitutional court and its public broadcasters. It appointed pro-government figures to the constitutional court and curbed its powers, making vetoes of government legislation more difficult. The government has also introduced measures that would give it greater control over public broadcasters. They are seen by the governing Law and Justice Party as dominated by figures sympathetic to the former Civic Platform-led government.[36] This politicization of the constitutional court and of the media echoes similar laws introduced by Viktor Orbán, Prime Minister and leader of the right-wing Fidesz party in Hungary. In response to these developments, the European Commission has indicated that it may initiate proceedings against Poland for violating some of the EU's basic laws. In 2014, the Dutchman Frans Timmermans, Vice President of the European Commission, spoke about the dangers of 'backsliding' in Eastern Europe, referring to a weakening in support for democracy following EU accession in 2004.

It is curious to hear European officials warn about the erosion of democratic standards in countries that have gone through a decade-long EU accession process, the main goal of which was the strengthening of democracy in the region. This 'backsliding' is rarely directly connected to the EU enlargement process itself, but the contemporary crisis of liberal democracy in Eastern Europe today cannot be dissociated from the EU's expansion into Eastern Europe. There are many different reasons for this crisis of democracy. The experience of transition from a command to a market economy led rapidly to new forms of social stratification in Eastern European societies. The old welfare state of the Soviet era, where job security was guaranteed and housing was provided by the state, disappeared, as did state support for many firms. State-sponsored farms also collapsed, with a significant impact upon rural communities. As these new social problems developed, the power of the old communist elite reasserted itself. Many members of the government in the pre-1989 era were reincarnated as post-communist politicians, forming parties with new names and new logos. This recycling of the elite is what angers figures such as Orbán in Hungary and Jarosław Kaczyński in Poland. They see it as evidence of how former communists still hold power behind the scenes and why the state apparatus needs to be purged.

Social movements, such as Solidarity in Poland, embraced marketization and privatization in the 1990s. This resulted in the curious situation whereby a movement set up by trade unions supported job cuts and the deregulation of the labour market. Solidarity also aligned itself with right-wing groups and marginalized the discussion of social or economic issues in favour of talking about religion.[37] The losers of transition have therefore had little by way of a political voice in recent years and have turned to parties of the right as a way of expressing their anger. These factors are at the heart of the current feelings of political disenchantment in Eastern Europe, but EU enlargement has magnified the gap between citizens and their government. The transition era, which lasted roughly from 1989 to 2005, was one of dramatic social and political change. However, many of these changes could not be politically debated and the direction of change could not be contested by citizens because of the strong association between transition and EU membership.

This association had the effect of censoring political criticisms and silencing any opposition to transition policies. National elites of the candidate states encouraged the connection between EU membership and transition policies largely because it made their job of governing much easier. A member of the Czech negotiating team with the EU remarked in 2004 that they felt some regret at the fact that their country was now a member of the EU. It would make the task of governing so much more difficult.[38] In the face of such cynicism, it is hardly surprising that Czech politics has been marked by the rise of anti-establishment figures. In 2011, one of the Czech Republic's richest businessmen, Andrej Babiš, founded the movement ANO, which means 'Yes' in Czech and also stands for 'Action for Dissatisfied Citizens'. In 2013, ANO became the second largest bloc in the country's Parliament and Babiš is today finance minister. His popularity rests on the frustrations of many Czechs with their own politicians. Babiš was elected on the back of promises to tackle corruption and to bring his business acumen to bear on the management of Czech politics. His critics call him 'Babisconi', an allusion to the former Italian premier Silvio Berlusconi which makes the similarities between Eastern and Western Europe all the more striking. The EU has done nothing to bridge this growing gap between societies and governments which, since 2004, has been the source of such disenchantment. Far from encouraging domestic political debates during the accession process, the EU was happier dealing with compliant teams of national experts than with truculent parliamentarians concerned about the erosion of national sovereignty.

The irony is that EU enlargement has, after all, had the effect of uniting Western and Eastern Europe for the first time. It is, as the historian Perry Anderson has observed, 'a historical accomplishment of the first order'.[39] However, the union that has been created is not one that its architects had aimed for. What stands out about the crisis of democracy in Eastern Europe is how similar it is to the crisis of representation in Western Europe that we saw in Chapter 4. Disenchantment with political establishments, a widespread loss of trust in politics, a growing interest in anti-establishment populist movements, the articulation of social problems as matters of religion and culture – these are all the same themes that preoccupy commentators in Western European states. Enlargement has been the basis for a new European union, but it is a union of citizens disillusioned with their political leaders and sceptical about the ability of their political systems to deliver on their promises.

CHAPTER 6

Could the EU Become a Superpower?

Groundhog Europe

In the film *Groundhog Day*, Bill Murray plays a miserly, mis-anthropic weatherman who finds himself stuck in a time loop and forced to relive the same day time after time in the provincial town of Punxsutawney, western Pennsylvania. The European Union's role in international affairs has an undeniable 'Groundhog Day' quality to it. The clichés used to describe the EU's role in world politics have been remarkably stable throughout nearly half a century of EU foreign policy.

One of the most popular clichés is that the EU 'does not speak with one voice'. This refers to the fact that EU member states often disagree on foreign policy issues, and so the position taken by the EU, which must please everyone, is watered down and weak. Former European Commissioner for External Relations Chris Patten explained that a truly common policy would 'imply either a denial of the bonds that create a national sense of community or the fraying of these bonds and their replacement by a wider sense of loy-alty and attachment'. The latter may sound nice, but it wasn't happening, according to Patten. 'For the foreseeable future', he wrote back in 2005, 'Europe will have twenty-five foreign ministers and twenty-five foreign ministries committed to trying to work together, but not doing themselves out of a job.'[1] Fast-forward ten years and the same observation can be made, though with a few more foreign ministers involved in EU foreign policy-making. In 2013, the foreign policy expert Anand Menon remarked that 'divergences between the interests of Member States anxious to retain their foreign policy prerogatives' remained a fundamental problem of EU foreign policy.[2] The Ukraine crisis, which broke out when Russia annexed the Crimea after the collapse of the Yanukovych government in February 2014, has been interpreted as another foreign policy opportunity that the EU failed to seize. The EU has been 'unable to speak with one voice' regretted the Chatham House fellow Orysia Lutsevych.[3] 'Once again national interests undermine Europe,' warned the *Financial Times* columnist Wolfgang Münchau darkly.[4]

A second cliché which commentators use when discussing the EU's foreign policy is that Europe 'punches below its weight'. This implies that the EU's 'weight', measured in terms of its population of 500 million and its very high GDP per capita, is not translated into a powerful foreign policy punch. The EU is, to use another popular cliché, 'an economic giant but a political dwarf': it has economic and demographic power but no corresponding military power. Put in another way, the EU has plenty of soft power but not much hard power. As Ivan Krastev and Mark Leonard quipped in an article in *Foreign Affairs* in 2015, faced with Putin's determination to retain influence in Ukraine, 'the EU's soft power proved to be very soft indeed'.[5] Optimists reply that a strong foreign policy today need not rely on military force, but this is increasingly less convincing in a world of Islamic State and Russian belligerence.

Yet another cliché is that the EU fails to 'match rhetoric with reality'. There are many variations on this theme: the EU 'talks the talk but doesn't walk the walk'; it 'talked a passable game' but 'no one got their shorts dirty'.[6] 'All words and no action' sums up this view. The most famous instance came in 1991, when violence broke out in Slovenia, presaging a more dramatic unravelling of the entire Yugoslav federation. European heads of government were in Luxembourg for a European Council meeting. Observing events in the Balkans, it struck them as a perfect opportunity for the EC to prove itself in foreign policy. Six months earlier, the Community had been unable to pull itself together in response to Saddam Hussein's invasion of Kuwait and the subsequent Gulf War was an American-led affair. This time, they believed, it would be different. Speaking to journalists, the veteran Luxembourgian foreign minister Jacques Poos announced that 'if one problem can be solved by the Europeans, it is the Yugoslav problem'. 'This is a European country,' he continued, in the manner of someone unaware that they have already said too much, 'and it is not up to the Americans. It is not up to anyone else.'[7] For all of his promises, the EC did very little. In fact, rivalries between member states fanned the flames of conflict. German public opinion pushed Chancellor Helmut Kohl to break EC ranks and unilaterally recognize the independence of Croatia and Slovenia. French and British diplomats viewed this as a bid for power by a newly united Germany keen to extend its influence deep into the Balkans.[8]

One final cliché tends to be the most popular. It is the notion that the EU is at a 'crossroads' in foreign policy, what others call a 'make-or-break' moment. Here, the EU is usually faced with a historic choice of some kind. EU foreign policy commentator Richard Youngs remarked in his 2010 book that if the EU didn't get its act together, it would be consigned to 'global irrelevance'.[9] The meaning of these 'crossroads' has evolved over time. Back in the early 1990s, the context was the end of the Cold War and the future of the Atlantic alliance. Europe, at a crossroads, could either remain dependent upon the United States for its security or break out on its own, forming its own security alliance for a much-changed continent. The war in Kosovo in 1999 was another 'make-or-break' moment when Europeans chose to rely on US airpower to bomb Slobodan Milošević into submission. The impact of the Eurozone crisis on EU defence spending was described as another critical turning point. In 2012, the war in Libya was seen as a Rubicon-crossing moment for the EU's foreign policy. Virtually every crisis is a watershed moment for the EU, a time when Europe must step up to its global responsibilities. The war in Ukraine, two decades since Jacques Poos' fateful words, was described in the media as 'the hour of Europe'.[10] A recent agreement between Iran and the West on Iran's nuclear capabilities, in which EU representatives played an important role, was hailed as a turning point for the EU. The Iran deal was an historic opportunity, wrote Ellie Geranmayeh of the European Council on Foreign

Relations, for Europe to assert its status as an independent power.[11]

It is the recycling of these clichés that gives the EU's foreign policy its Groundhog Day quality. How did the EU get stuck in this time loop and might it find a way out? Before answering these questions, we have to consider first of all what EU foreign policy is. Though it exists, it is not commonly discussed or even known about.

Ad hoc coalitions of the willing

Describing what it felt like to return to the UK after four years spent as the European Commissioner for External Relations, Chris Patten recounts an anecdote told by three-times British Prime Minister Stanley Baldwin.[12] Baldwin was travelling home to Worcestershire on the train at some point in the 1930s and someone sitting opposite him asked, 'Weren't you at Harrow in the '80s?' Baldwin answered that he was. 'Thought so, so was I!' came the reply. 'So what have you been doing with yourself since then?' asked the curious but obviously poorly informed passenger. Patten identifies with the story, saying that he felt the same after returning from Brussels. EU foreign policy, he implied, was marked by anonymity.

One reason for this is its complexity. A joke that regularly makes it around the EU is the one about what number you can call when you want to get through to Europe. This was reportedly the question former Secretary of State Henry Kissinger asked back in the 1970s. The answer, in the most recent version of the joke (there have been many) was that there is now a single number, but when a US Secretary of State calls, they get a recorded voice, saying 'for French foreign policy press 1 . . . for British foreign policy press 2 . . .' and so on.[13] At the time, this joke was partly intended as a criticism of the EU's foreign policy chief, Baroness Catherine Ashton, whose work habits ran up against the chauvinism of some of the Brussels press corps. The long-time correspondent for *Libération* in Brussels, Jean Quatremer, wrote an outraged blog post where he 'revealed' that Ashton would leave Brussels on Friday evening and spend her weekends in London with her family.[14] An unforgivable habit, in his view, no better than sleeping on the job.

The EU's foreign policy is often the work of a small handful of member states, not of the EU as a whole. When Russia invaded Georgia in 2008, French President Nicolas Sarkozy, backed by his energetic foreign minister Bernard Kouchner, led the EU response. In their dealings with Russia, Sarkozy and Kouchner thought of themselves as envoys for the rest of the EU. In a technical sense they were, as France held the rotating presidency of the European Council at that moment. But their behaviour left other member states grumbling about typical French grandstanding. Subsequent accounts of the events have raised doubts about the effectiveness of France's mediation.[15] In the case of the negotiations with Iran, the EU has been represented by the 'E3', a term which sounds like a robot from *Star Wars* but in fact refers to the United Kingdom, France and Germany.

In contrast to most other areas of the EU's business, in security and defence it is acceptable if only a minority of member states act together. There are even specific provisions in the EU treaties for this, known as 'permanent structured cooperation', but rather than go down that route, leaders often prefer ad hoc coalitions of the willing. The crisis in Ukraine saw both France and Germany take a lead, with Angela Merkel and François Hollande travelling to meet and negotiate with Vladimir Putin. David Cameron stayed at home. In Libya in 2011, France and the United Kingdom took the lead in intervening to depose Colonel Gaddafi, with the United States saying it would 'lead from behind'. In this instance, there was no pretence that France and Britain were 'standing in' for the rest of the EU. Germany had abstained when the United Nations Security Council voted on Resolution 1973 on air strikes and Libya eventually became a NATO mission (though less than a third of NATO members took part in it). Many observed at the time that the EU's security and defence policy 'went missing in action during the Libya crisis'.[16]

Turf wars

While such ad hoc coalitions of member states are a common feature of the EU's foreign policy, this is a policy area with its own dedicated personnel, procedures and institutions. If we read the EU's treaties closely, the most important figure is the High Representative for Foreign Affairs and Security Policy. This post is currently held by the Italian centre-left politician Federica Mogherini. Her predecessor was the British peer Baroness Ashton. The first person in the post was the Spaniard Javier Solana. Foreign policy experience is not a prerequisite for this job: Ashton had virtually none, Mogherini a bit more but still relatively little compared to others who were in the running for the job. Only Solana had a strong foreign policy CV, having been Spain's foreign minister in the early 1990s and Secretary General of NATO from 1995 to 1999. Appointments to this role are political and being in the right place at the right time has a lot to do with it. After the 2014 European parliamentary elections, Italian MEPs dominated the Socialists and Democrats group in the Parliament. According to Italian premier Matteo Renzi, this meant he was 'owed' a top EU job and so he put Mogherini forward as 'his candidate'.

The job of High Representative is one of the most demanding of EU top jobs and competes with the US Secretary of State in terms of air miles per year. It is also one of the best paid: when in office, Ashton was the second highest paid female politician in the world.[17] On an annual gross salary of £287,500 a year, she came in just behind Christine Lagarde, the head of the International Monetary Fund. The post used to be a more modest one. Foreign policy has always been the preserve of the Council of Ministers, not of the European Commission. As such, the job was tied to that of Secretary General of the Council of Ministers. This was Javier Solana's position when he was appointed as the first High Representative and it made sense that the figure representing the EU to the outside world would be able to benefit from all the policy expertise located within the Council secretariat. This post first appeared in the Treaty of Amsterdam of 1997 in order to give the EU more continuity in its foreign policy. Up until then, the only representative of member states was the rotating Presidency of the European Council. When a large member state held the presidency, such as France or Italy, foreign policy would be given considerable importance and resources. When smaller member states held the presidency, it was put on the back-burner. Having someone permanently in place, who ran the Council secretariat and was able to build long-term relationships with member states, was intended to give the EU greater clout.

As with many changes, improvements in one place can lead to problems elsewhere. The difficulty with the new High Representative role was that it rubbed up against the role of the European Commission in foreign affairs. Though foreign policy has generally been a matter for member states, the Commission has long had its own directorate-general for external relations, known as DG RELEX. The Commissioner running DG RELEX oversaw a sizeable budget and was responsible for policies such as the EU's enlargement and its relations with countries further afield, known as the EU's Neighbourhood Policy. Often, the High Representative and the European Commissioner for External Relations would compete with one another. For outsiders, it sometimes wasn't clear who the 'official' representative of the EU was. Jealous of its role in EU foreign policy, the Commission would carefully guard its mandate, leading to numerous turf wars between the Commission and the Council of Ministers. The Commission has even taken the Council to court, as it did in a case relating to Council assistance to the Economic Community of West African States. Believing the Council had overstepped its powers, the Commission took the case to the European Court of Justice and won.[18]

In order to eliminate these turf wars, the Treaty of Lisbon

of 2009 introduced important changes to the EU foreign policy-making machine. The High Representative job was blown up into enormous, superhuman proportions, while the Commission's role in foreign policy was clipped. DG RELEX was wound up and absorbed into a new institution, the European External Action Service (EEAS). This body was set up as an amalgam of former Commission officials, officials from within the Council secretariat and officials from member states sent to Brussels on temporary postings. The boss of this new institution is the High Representative and the outgoing director-general of DG RELEX was appointed as Chief Operating Officer of the EEAS. Another new role for the High Representative was the vice-presidency of the European Commission. The idea behind this change was that the activities of the Commission would be better coordinated with those of the Council because one person was representing both institutions. Another view might be that the Council fox was being let into the Commission chicken coop. Finally, under the terms of the Lisbon Treaty, the influential General Affairs and External Relations Council was split into two separate bodies, the General Affairs Council and the Foreign Affairs Council. The High Representative would chair the latter, which is made up of foreign and defence ministers.

This beefed-up High Representative role has not been an unmitigated success, far from it. One problem has been the creation of another new post, the permanent President of the European Council. Formally speaking, this person should only assist the High Representative in foreign affairs. Their main task is to coordinate the work of the European Council itself. However, as the President is also the face of the EU to the outside world, the role has an inescapable foreign policy dimension to it. Some have suggested that because the current President of the European Council, Donald Tusk, is Polish, he can take a lead on Eastern European and Russia-related matters. Others have resisted this, saying it will only undermine the High Representative. Tusk himself has taken an active interest in foreign policy. On his first day as President of the European Council, he telephoned US President Barack Obama. Within a couple of days of starting his job, he had met with the Afghan President and the NATO Secretary General and had spoken over the phone with the Chinese President.[19] Tusk's predecessor Herman Van Rompuy had concentrated on economic issues as his term coincided with the height of the Eurozone's sovereign debt crisis. Tusk may have more opportunity to involve himself in foreign policy, but how this will fit with the role of the High Representative is less clear.

At one level below these political figures lies the EU's foreign policy-making machinery, dominated by officials and national diplomats. The Political and Security Committee, known by its French acronym as '*le* COPS', is made up of national officials who have the rank of ambassador. Their role is to coordinate the positions of member states, ensuring that there is agreement when foreign ministers arrive in Brussels for Foreign Affairs Council meetings. Below them are armies of officials, within the foreign offices of member states, in the permanent representations of member states in Brussels and in the External Action Service.

Dying for Europe

Where does the deployment of military power fit into all of this? What, exactly, does the EU *do*? People talk about a European army as if it were something that existed or is just around the corner. The British, in particular, are suspicious of any efforts to integrate defence capabilities in Europe. The truth is that the formation of a single European army is as far away as it has ever been. Defence cooperation in the EU remains sporadic and limited. There was not a single discussion of defence issues at European Council meetings between 2008 and 2013, in spite of all that happened in global politics during this period.

The most concrete elements of the EU's foreign policy are the international missions. Since 2003, the EU has conducted thirty-two such missions, all of which have gone under the heading of the EU's security and defence policy. The number of ongoing missions is sixteen and involves the deployment of around 6,000 people.[20] This may sound like a lot but the EU's missions are modest and on a small scale. To put them in perspective, at the height of its involvement in Afghanistan, the UK had 9,500 troops in the country. Germany had almost 1,000 troops in Afghanistan at the end of 2015, while Poland sent 2,000 troops to Iraq in 2003. The largest EU mission is Operation Atalanta, an anti-piracy mission operating off the coast of Somalia, employing 1,719. However, contributors to this mission include a number of non-EU member states, such as Norway, Serbia, Montenegro, Ukraine and New Zealand. One of the smallest EU missions is the border-monitoring operation in Libya, which employs around seventeen international staff. The average size of the EU's missions taking place in 2015 was 376.[21]

The EU's own missions are both civilian and military. Civilian missions involve activities such as mentoring, advising and training, often done by police or customs officers rather than by soldiers. The EU's civilian missions also include monitoring of ceasefires and overseeing the implementation of agreements. The EU monitors the Rafah border crossing point in the Gaza Strip and the borders between Georgia and the breakaway regions of Abkhazia and South Ossetia. In Kosovo, the EU takes a more direct role in running the country. Since 2008, its rule of law mission, known as EULEX, has had executive responsibilities in the areas of war crimes, organized crime and high-level corruption. Part of the EU's Common Security and Defence Policy (CSDP), there is no actual defence element in these missions; they are conducted in times of peace.

The EU's military missions themselves also fall short of actual war-fighting.[22] The EU's only combat mission in the last five years was in the Central African Republic. Since its president was overthrown in 2013, by a mainly Muslim rebel alliance, the Central African Republic has been mired in violent confrontations between Christian and Muslim groups. The EU mission began in 2014 and was terminated at the end of March 2015. Though a combat mission, every effort was made to make it risk-free. It was small in scale (750 troops) and the troops were sent to two districts in the capital, Bangui, and the airport. A clear exit strategy was identified from the beginning, with the mission to be handed over to

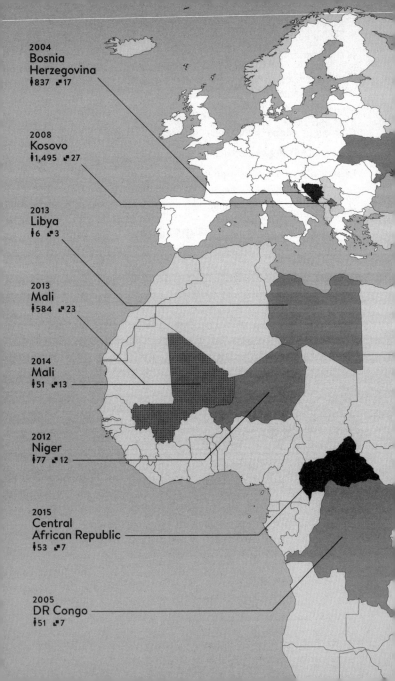

2004
Bosnia
Herzegovina
837 17

2008
Kosovo
1,495 27

2013
Libya
6 3

2013
Mali
584 23

2014
Mali
51 13

2012
Niger
77 12

2015
Central
African Republic
53 7

2005
DR Congo
51 7

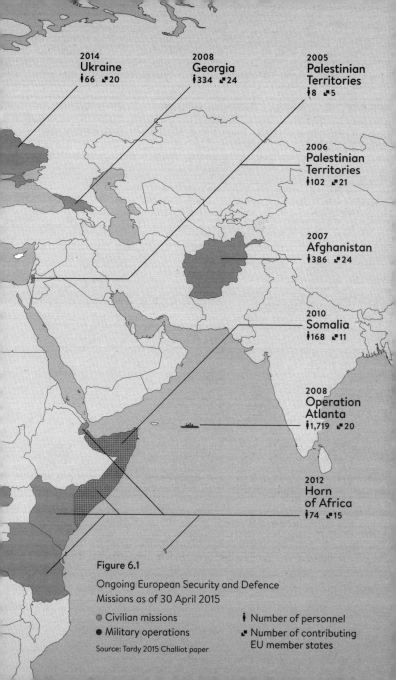

2014
Ukraine
♦66 ◾20

2008
Georgia
♦334 ◾24

2005
Palestinian
Territories
♦8 ◾5

2006
Palestinian
Territories
♦102 ◾21

2007
Afghanistan
♦386 ◾24

2010
Somalia
♦168 ◾11

2008
Operation
Atlanta
♦1,719 ◾20

2012
Horn
of Africa
♦74 ◾15

Figure 6.1

Ongoing European Security and Defence
Missions as of 30 April 2015

● Civilian missions
● Military operations

♦ Number of personnel
◾ Number of contributing
EU member states

Source: Tardy 2015 Challiot paper

the African Union (it was handed over to the UN in the end). In spite of these efforts, six separate meetings had to be organized before member states could be convinced to make the required contributions to the missions. In the end, France provided the majority of the troops. Remarkably, the second largest contributor to this mission was Georgia, which was not even a member of the EU. This mission reported one death, the French corporal Heiarii Moana, but as a result of malaria. To date, no soldier has died fighting under an EU flag. In fact, the only reported deaths associated with an EU flag are those of civilians – Ukrainian protestors in Kiev who were shot by their own government.

In a 2015 paper, EU security analyst Thierry Tardy wrote that the EU's missions should be considered 'sub-strategic', which means that they have been small-scale and have not had a major impact on the recipient states. 'Most CSDP operations', he concluded, 'are too small or short-term to signify an EU strategic involvement.'[23] A number of opportunities for missions identified by the External Action Service have been ignored by member states. Since 2010 almost all the operations have struggled to get the necessary resources together. The EU's battle groups, a term which refers to the EU's ability to respond to a crisis rapidly by sending units of 1,500 troops out into the field within fifteen days of deciding on the mission, have never been deployed.

The EU has extensive foreign policy instruments at its disposal. In spite of that, it fails to break through into the world of power politics. How can we explain this combination of continuous activity and minimal influence? The answer lies in the EU's member states. The EU's role in international politics reflects the ambitions and desires of its members. And the difficulties the EU has in foreign policy come from the fact that these members, in particular those who retain the greatest military clout, have steadily retreated from international politics.

Europe's retreat from power

The British diplomat Robert Cooper once wrote that the events of 1989 represented not just the end of the Cold War, but also signalled the end of 'the political systems of three centuries: the balance of power and the imperial urge'.[24] In a sense, he was right. Mechanisms such as the balance of power, the launching and expansion of empires, and other features of the modern international system all rest upon an idea of nation-states as self-interested and egotistical, driven by a desire for supremacy, willing to fight and risk the lives of their citizens in order to achieve their goals. What Cooper was suggesting was that with 1989 came the end of this kind of state. If there is no ambition in Europe to shape international politics and to play the game of power politics, it is no wonder that EU foreign policy falls short of doing so. It simply fills the gap left by the retreat of Europe's powers. Where Cooper was wrong was that this kind of state did not just disappear overnight with the fall of the Berlin Wall and the disappearance of the Soviet Union. The changes had been taking place well before 1989.

The figures tell an interesting story about Europe's retreat from power politics. European states generally spend little on defence today and what remains of their armed forces are less oriented towards active combat than ever before. Germany made a large contribution to the International Security Assistance force (ISAF) mission in Afghanistan, with around 4,400 troops in the country in August 2013. However, they were all sent to the peaceful north and forbidden from undertaking any combat activities.[25] Other European contributions were so insignificant that it is difficult to know whether they were intended as a snub. The Irish sent seven soldiers, Luxembourg sent nine, Austria sent three. Defence spending by Europe's main powers has been either stagnant or in terminal decline. As a proportion of GDP, defence spending has been more or less constant between 2003 and 2012, but as actual spending in real terms it has fallen steeply. France saw a decrease of 3.3 per cent between 2003 and 2012; Germany and Italy saw a fall of 1.9 per cent for the same period.[26] The UK saw an increase of 4.9 per cent, but this figure is misleading. UK defence spending is skewered towards military equipment as a way of supporting domestic industry. Much of the UK's defence budget is also dedicated to its nuclear arsenal. Estimates are that Trident will consume a third of the UK's entire budget for military equipment in the coming decades, unless Jeremy Corbyn has his way and scraps the deterrent.[27]

The European Union Institute of Security Studies runs a military expenditure index, which found that defence spending in the EU as a whole had fallen by 13.6 per cent in real terms since 2007. Reductions in defence spending in Southern European states have been even more dramatic, up to 70 per cent in places. These figures are not consequences of the economic crisis. In the UK, defence spending remained constant between 1955 and 1979, meaning that relative to other policy areas it has shrunk in importance. It accounted for 25.1 per cent of the total expenditure of the British state in the mid-1950s, falling to 10.9 per cent by end of the 1970s.[28] In the Netherlands, defence represented 18.3 per cent of the country's budget in 1960, but only 9.8 per cent in 1980. The steady increase in GDP over the course of the post-war period was thus matched by a steady decline in the proportion of that spent on defence.

Figures alone never tell the whole story and one can exaggerate the narrative of Europe's demilitarization. The EU's big four – the UK, France, Germany and Italy – are still very well armed. According to the Stockholm International Peace Research Institute (SIPRI), in 2014 France was fifth in the world in terms of defence spending, the UK sixth, Germany eighth and Italy twelfth. According to SIPRI again, these four EU states are all in the top ten in terms of arms exports: France is fourth, Germany fifth, the UK sixth and Italy ninth. Spain, which ranks eighth, also has a very significant arms export industry. In 2015, the French defence industry alone won 16 billion euros of overseas orders, providing a boost to its big military companies such as Dassault Aviation, DCNS, MBDA, Safran and Thales.[29] There is also some difference between Western and Eastern Europe. Poland bucks the trend of declining military budgets, its defence spending rising by 38 per cent in real terms between 2005 and 2014.[30] Some of this spending was as a result of an equipment modernization plan that will last until 2022, but Poland is also much closer to Ukraine and Russia than other EU member states. The Baltic States have also increased military spending since they joined NATO in 2004 but they were very heavily hit by the economic crisis of the late 2000s. Latvia cut its spending by 55 per cent between 2007 and 2012.

Europe's retreat from power politics goes deeper than just shrinking defence budgets. Demilitarization is also about culture and politics and the balance between civilian and military values within society. In his book *Where Have All the Soldiers Gone?*, the historian James Sheehan describes the changing place of conscription in post-1945 Western European societies. Historically, conscription played a key role in keeping military values at the heart of social life. The nation, as an idea, came with the French Revolution and the *levée en masse* – the decision to enrol ordinary French citizens into the army in order to defend the gains of the Revolution from external threats. From having been an activity carried out by paid professionals (mercenaries) and elites, fighting for one's country became from the late eighteenth century onwards a key pillar of citizenship itself. The nation was defined by an ability to represent itself to outside threats as an organized mass of armed citizens.

Conscription was generally maintained in Western Europe after 1945, though in the UK it lasted only until 1960. In France, it lasted much longer. The national service law of 1950 required that men serve eighteen months of active duty (later increased to thirty-six months) plus three years in the active reserve. They were also required to serve sixteen years in the non-active reserve and then eight years on standby. Winding down the French tradition of military service took some time, but by 1996 then-President Jacques Chirac had committed himself to creating a professional army.

Today, in France, all that remains is the 'day of defence and citizenship' – an obligation on all French nationals that involves short courses on the army itself and some first aid courses provided by the Red Cross. Elsewhere, the nature and obligations of conscription changed radically across the post-war period. The Dutch introduced regular hours, overtime and unionization into their conscript army, making the army a job like any other.[31] West Germany introduced conscription in 1956 in spite of widespread public hostility to the idea. However, the numbers opting for civilian rather than military service increased steadily – by the 1990s, almost one in two of those doing military service were choosing civilian tasks such as working in hospitals or schools.

Europe's retreat from power politics signals a profound transformation in the nature of European states and societies. The duty to fight and risk one's life for one's country no longer forms the basis of the present-day social contract in most European states. These states are welfare states, not warfare states. An overwhelming majority of citizens say they would never consider fighting for their country. A poll in 2014 found that only 29 per cent of French would be willing to fight for their country. Twenty-seven per cent of the British polled said they would and 18 per cent of Germans. More than two thirds of Italians said they would refuse to fight for their country. In the early twentieth century, the struggle between militarism and pacifism was a fundamental contest between very different sorts of values. In many circles, pacifism was considered an awful moral failure and famous pacifists such as Bertrand Russell were socially ostracized. Today, the social contract has been rewritten in terms of work and welfare. More stigma is attached to those who draw benefits while not working than to those who declare themselves unwilling to fight for their country were they ever asked to do so.

One reason for this change was the way the Cold War liberated Western European states from having to take control of their own security. The United States had encouraged European rearmament in the late 1940s and early 1950s as a way of freeing itself from the burden of its military presence in Europe, but with limited success. Building a common European defence ran up against French resistance to the idea of putting French soldiers under the authority of German officers. The French were also very reluctant to support US and British efforts at rebuilding the West German military. Memories of the Second World War were too fresh. Jean Monnet's biographer, François Duchêne, describes one meeting of European defence ministers in October 1950, where the Frenchman Jules Moch refused to support German rearmament. For the duration of the whole meeting, Madame Moch sat immobile behind her husband, dressed in black from head to foot. The Mochs' son had been tortured and killed by the Germans in the war.[32] Faced with these problems, the US maintained its commitment to European defence and strengthened the North Atlantic Treaty Organization (NATO). In 1955, West Germany was recognized as a fully independent sovereign state and joined NATO the same year. Channelling European security through NATO meant that the US took a lead in providing it. Not all were happy with this arrangement, and General de Gaulle took France out of NATO's high command in 1966. However, the alliance allowed Western European states to devote themselves more fully to civilian activities and to stoking the post-war economic boom.

The Cold War relieved many European governments of practical responsibility for their own self-defence while fitting these countries into a framework where war and confrontation were never far away. Though the flashpoints of the Cold War moved away from Europe from the late 1960s onwards, the dividing line of the Iron Curtain retained its importance. Even as late as 1986, enormous amounts of military hardware were located along this border. In East Germany alone, ninety-four divisions were stationed there, along with 30,000 tanks and 30,000 armoured personnel carriers. In West Germany, NATO had 9,000 tanks and 17,000 armoured personnel carriers. In addition to this were the thousands of tactical nuclear weapons, hundreds of thousands of tons of chemical agents and millions of tons of conventional arms.[33] The significance of 1989 and the collapse of the Soviet Union is not least that it meant much of this military hardware was moved out of Germany.

The key factor explaining the declining belligerence of European states is not to be found in international politics, however. It comes from domestic politics. The centrality of war in European society was a reflection of conflict between different ideologies and wars evolved in line with changes in ideological frameworks. Religiously motivated conflict gave way to class conflict. Nationalism as a mass phenomenon developed in response to class warfare and represented an attempt at preserving Europe's state system from this internationalist threat.[34] By 1945, these ideologies had begun to lose some of their power. Religion had become less central to social life and divisions between Catholics and Protestants no longer drove states to war against one another. The failure of the Bolshevik Revolution to export itself to the rest of Europe was a blow to those who had believed social change would only come through class war. In the inter-war period, radical left movements made little headway in Western Europe. Those voting on the left were absorbed into a patriotic and nationalistic anti-Nazi front that cemented an alliance between the left and the democratic capitalist state. Nationalism itself was dealt a historic blow by the Second World War and by the Nazi Party. The redefinition of the nation in exclusively racist terms, a far cry from the secular and universal idea of the nation coined in 1789, meant that after 1945 nationalism was inseparable from the horrors of the Third Reich.

By the 1950s, political life in Western Europe was no longer organized around a struggle to the death between the radical left and the nationalist and racist right. The framework of the market was broadly accepted, as was the idea of an interventionist state. It was this growing ideological moderation that explains Western Europe's slow retreat from the power politics and imperial urges of the nineteenth century. The great moral crusades and conflicts of past eras had given way to a widely endorsed post-war consensus. By the time 1989 came around, there was nothing left of the intra-European rivalries that had made war a way of life in Europe. That is why German reunification resulted in no real external conflict despite the fears many held at the time. The tearing down of the Berlin Wall did not end the political system of three centuries, as Robert Cooper suggested: that order had ended long before. The fall of the Wall merely revealed its absence to the rest of the world.

In search of identity

It would be a mistake to conclude that Europe's retreat from military power makes the EU's foreign policy irrelevant. On the contrary, there are a number of important roles that foreign policy plays in EU integration. The time-loop quality of EU foreign policy stems in part from the fact that many people are determined to think of EU foreign policy only in terms of the projection of military force across the world. Seen in those terms, EU foreign policy will always disappoint.

A key purpose of EU foreign policy is to give the EU some kind of identity, preferably one that distinguishes it from the other actors in the international system, especially states like the US, China and Russia. The EU's military missions, for example, are regularly used for this purpose. Too small to be of any real consequence for the countries concerned, they are nevertheless important for the EU itself. In Bosnia, the British general David Leakey recounted his experience of leading an EU mission. EUFOR Althea, launched in 2004, was the EU's third and most ambitious military mission. The EU was taking over from NATO in Bosnia and this was a mission high in symbolism for EU foreign policy enthusiasts. Leakey felt that his instructions were rather vague and so he asked the then High Representative, Javier Solana, for more detailed advice. Solana replied that Leakey should just try to 'make a difference' and do something 'new and distinct'.[35] Far from reassured, Leakey found himself on the ground in Bosnia, looking for something that his soldiers could do. Concerned that they would get restless, he fell upon the idea of tackling organized crime. Over time, EUFOR Althea was celebrated as an example of how the EU does innovative things with traditional military personnel. Leakey was congratulated for his ability to lead a mission that was neither just military nor civilian, but both.

Trying to identify the EU's unique contribution to international politics, and in this way to build up its own sense of self, has become the main activity of an army of analysts. When describing Europe as a power in the world, we have a dizzying array of qualifying adjectives that are meant to highlight how the EU is different from nation-states. The EU has been described as a 'transformative power', a 'normative power', an 'ethical power', a 'responsible power' and a 'postmodern power'. The EU has even been hailed as a 'metrosexual power', making it the David Beckham of world politics.[36] When we analyse the EU's foreign policy, we should think more in terms of what contribution it is making to the development of the EU's identity and less in terms of the difference it is making to the world at large.

Making Europe more popular

Another important purpose of the EU's foreign policy is to make the bloc more popular with its citizens. Consistently in opinion polls there is strong support for a more active EU in international affairs. When voters rejected the

Constitutional Treaty in France and Holland in 2005, it was suggested that a stronger foreign policy could be a way of boosting public support for the EU. In a speech three months after the 'No' votes, Javier Solana declared that he was 'personally convinced that the CFSP [Common Foreign and Security Policy] has its role to play in the reconquering of public opinion in favour of the European project'.[37] This same argument has been made in efforts to win over a more Eurosceptic British audience. In 2000, Tony Blair gave a speech at the Polish Stock Exchange, in which he argued that Europe should become a superpower rather than a superstate. Blair's vision was of the EU pursuing a foreign policy focused on humanitarian intervention, of the kind undertaken by NATO in Kosovo a year earlier. Having made peace in Europe, he argued that the EU should start projecting power beyond the borders of Europe, particularly in places that lacked democratic government. In his speech, Blair was clear that he felt this kind of democracy-promoting EU would help boost its popularity.

This role for EU foreign policy has declined, particularly since 2008 when priorities shifted to the economic terrain. Saving the euro has become more of a priority than projecting European power beyond its borders. In a late 2015 Eurobarometer poll, only 6 per cent of respondents considered Europe's influence in the world to be one of the EU's two top priorities.[38] Unsurprisingly, given the timing, immigration and terrorism topped the list of concerns, with the economy, unemployment and the state of national public finances following.

Public support for EU foreign policy has depended on the

vague and general nature of the questions being asked. Few citizens of EU member states actively wish the EU to have *less* influence in the world. Public dissatisfaction with national foreign policy is also a common reason for looking more favourably towards the EU. Those public intellectuals who have issued calls for the EU to become a global power have tended to do so in the hope that this would mean Europe could begin to challenge American power and hegemony. As the German philosopher Jürgen Habermas argued in 2009, 'only a European Union with an effective foreign policy . . . could promote an alternative to the dominant Washington Consensus'.[39] The modesty of its actions is what enables EU foreign policy to enjoy broad public support. Were the EU to become engaged in foreign policy actions that had significant consequences for both the EU itself and the countries in which it was involved, intervention in Syria for instance or sending troops in Ukraine to fight the Russians, public support for EU foreign policy would be put to the test.

Conclusion

There is little likelihood of the EU becoming a superpower any time soon. It will remain stuck in its time loop, with people looking to Europe to act and being disappointed at its inability to do so. The EU's complex institutional architecture devoted to foreign policy-making provides member states with a convincing story about how active they are in international affairs. From one crisis to another, foreign ministers congregate in Brussels and agree on common statements delivered with great seriousness to the global media.

This activity is a substitute for real action. It reflects a retreat from power by Europe's member states, which is the culmination of a long-standing process of historical change. Europe's big four – the United Kingdom, France, Germany and Italy – are still big spenders on defence and have domestic arms industries with a global reach. However, they are no longer major powers in the international system. European societies are no longer founded upon principles of militarism and war. Military academies such as Sandhurst in the UK and Saint-Cyr in France retain prestige, but they are no longer the training ground for the countries' elites that they once were. This political and cultural demilitarization of European society has come from the winding down of the ideological battles that once marked the continent. The EU's foreign policy serves to fill this gap and to hide Europe's retreat from power.

The EU Versus Democracy

The Varoufakis puzzle

Yanis Varoufakis was appointed finance minister shortly after Syriza's victory in the January 2015 general elections in Greece. His political experience was minimal: he was an academic economist and enthusiastic blogger who had been the President of the Black Students' Alliance at the University of Essex in the 1970s.[1] What he lacked in experience he made up for in self-confidence. Varoufakis quickly set to work to try to convince other European countries that it was time for a new approach to Greece. He believed it was a delusion to think that the EU could provide more credit to Greece and expect that the country would pay back these billions of euros. Varoufakis labelled this the policy of 'extend and pretend', arguing that, instead, Greece needed significant debt relief.

In early 2015, there was a lot of sympathy with Varoufakis's arguments. Institutions such as the International Monetary Fund made positive remarks about debt relief. Big countries, like France and Italy, were receptive to the Greek anti-austerity message. Yet a few months later, Greece's creditors told the Greek Prime Minister Alexis Tsipras that negotiations could only continue if Yanis Varoufakis had no part whatsoever to play in them. What had changed in so short a time and why did Varoufakis's peers want so much to get rid of him?

The antipathy felt towards Varoufakis was captured at a press conference held in Athens in January 2015. Varoufakis and Jeroen Dijsselbloem, Dutch finance minister and head of the Eurogroup, were addressing journalists after a meeting. The Greeks had come to dislike intensely the shadowy 'Troika', a group of three institutions representing Greece's main creditors: the International Monetary Fund, the European Commission and the European Central Bank. In the press conference, Varoufakis said that Greece would only continue negotiating with these institutions individually, but not together as the Troika. Dijsselbloem sat for a moment, waiting to hear the translation. As soon as it came through, the tall Dutchman stood up and turned to leave. Varoufakis stood up as well and offered Dijsselbloem his hand. With visible reluctance, the Dutchman took it, but at the same time whispered into Varoufakis's ear, 'you just killed the Troika'.[2]

Theories abound about why things went so sour. Some complain that Varoufakis lectured other finance ministers as if they were his students in an economics class. Others suggest that it was his iconoclasm and glamour that drew the ire of his colleagues. Dashing around Athens on a motorbike, looking well toned and tanned, turning up for a meeting at 10 Downing Street in a hunting jacket, and being photographed in *Paris Match* with his good-looking wife – no other Eurogroup finance minister had the same sort of panache.

The most convincing explanation is less to do with

personalities and more about institutions. The Eurozone's finance ministers eventually forced Varoufakis out because he violated the basic etiquette of the Eurogroup and challenged its ideological consensus. The Eurogroup is an informal body, with almost no legal existence. The only reference to it is a short protocol in the EU treaties (Protocol 14), consisting of two articles which do not tell us what role the Eurogroup should play other than to bring finance ministers together on an informal basis to discuss Eurozone-related matters.[3] Though made up of politicians, the Eurogroup is curiously apolitical. Etiquette requires that national interests be left at the door. It is a deliberative and collaborative body that aims to solve problems. Its ability to do so comes from an ideological consensus, upheld by member states, regarding the purpose of the Eurozone and the rules governing it. Finance ministers are bound by a sense of loyalty to each other and what goes on behind the closed doors remains secret.

Varoufakis broke almost every one of these informal rules. He was, as the political scientist Jan-Werner Müller has put it, a 'vandal in the engine room of the EU'.[4] Varoufakis understood himself as a representative of the Greek people and he treated the Eurogroup as a place of formal negotiation between states, not as an informal and deliberative group composed of like-minded individuals united by a shared purpose. He stood out like a sore thumb, refusing to sign off on amended texts until he had spoken to his Prime Minister and consulted the Greek Parliament. Perhaps his greatest sin, however, was to break the etiquette around secrecy. Varoufakis would regularly post on his blog the speeches he gave in the Eurogroup and he even recorded meetings on his mobile phone. He claims to have made the recordings in order to report more accurately the content of meetings to Alexis Tsipras and the Greek Cabinet. One suspects he did so in order to protect himself against his critics. When the *New York Times* ran a story saying that Varoufakis had been insulted by other finance ministers at a particularly confrontational meeting of the Eurogroup in Riga in April 2015, Varoufakis responded by saying that it was nonsense and that he could prove it as he had recordings of the meeting. The *New York Times* story disappeared, but there were howls of indignation at the idea that these private meetings had been recorded by one of its participants.

Varoufakis became a *persona non grata* because he tried to transform the EU's secret deliberations into an open political debate about the future of the Eurozone. By presenting himself as a direct and uncompromising representative of the Greek people, other finance ministers ended up looking as if they were putting the interests of the Eurozone ahead of the interests of their own populations.

Europe's impasse

The most important lesson of the Varoufakis saga is that life in the Eurozone involves pitting the survival of the euro against the wishes of national democracies. The Greeks forcefully rejected the bail-out agreement presented to them in a referendum in early July 2015. And yet, their Prime Minister accepted a new loan agreement that was even tougher than the one voted on. This notion of European institutions at loggerheads with national democracy gained traction during the euro-crisis because it tapped into a wider sentiment about the place of democracy in the EU.

A lesson of the Eurozone has been that since countries cannot devalue their currencies in order to boost competitiveness, they must achieve the same effect by pushing down wages and prices. These strategies are reminiscent of another fixed exchange rate regime, the gold standard. The difference is that the gold standard was in place before the countries taking part in it became fully democratic, and it was abandoned when democratization had gone far enough to make the policies demanded by membership of it impossible to push through via democratic procedures. The euro makes similar demands, and in Greece there came a point when the population just said it could not take it anymore. And yet it was ignored by its own government and by the rest of the Eurozone. In Italy, Silvio Berlusconi was pushed out in a soft European-led coup in a bid to ensure that the country would implement the reforms demanded by its membership of the Eurozone.

The EU has reached an impasse. Policy-makers, experts and commentators will say, almost unanimously, that in order to solve the problems facing the EU, more integration is necessary. According to economists, the Eurozone crisis has revealed the problem of having a single monetary policy alongside decentralized fiscal policy. The answer lies in a fiscal union: a European finance ministry or treasury, capable of determining how much governments tax and spend. In response to the migration crisis, many have called for the transformation of Frontex, the EU's border security agency, into a pan-European border police force with authority to act on the external border of all EU member states. We are regularly told that powers currently held by national governments need to be fully invested in a central authority. And yet, there is no public support for these changes. Public opinion on EU integration may change in the future, but for the moment there is no appetite for large transfers of sovereignty to the European Commission or any other EU institution. Germany is resisting the idea of a common deposit insurance scheme in the EU's banking union so as to avoid guaranteeing deposits of savers from across the EU. Greeks are unwilling to give up control over their own borders to an EU agency. The German sociologist Claus Offe has said that Europe, under these conditions, is 'entrapped': unable to move forward, it cannot move backwards either.[5]

One way of escaping this trap is to develop policies against the wishes of Europe's populations; in sum, to ignore them. Though unlikely to be done in an obvious way, the EU is well versed in undertaking what the Italian political scientist Giandomenico Majone has called 'integration by stealth'.[6] The EU's legislative complexity lends itself to this method, as an idea rejected at one point in time can often reappear in slightly different packaging a bit later. It can be proposed by a different institution and under a different procedure so that the formal requirements for adopting it are less constraining.

Unwilling to embrace this cynical strategy of subterfuge, a number of people have called for the democratization of Europe as a whole. Rather than see a clash between Europe and democracy, why not raise democracy to the European level? This has been the argument of prominent public intellectuals, such as Jürgen Habermas in Germany, and many others. They accept the time is not ripe for building a federal European state. But they suggest that some sort of supranational democracy is possible. Others have called for the creation of a European constitutional assembly, tasked with writing a European constitution. Yanis Varoufakis himself has opted for this route. As well as having provoked the hatred of the Eurogroup, Varoufakis has also become the least favourite person of many Greeks. In the time-honoured fashion of pursuing a political career in Europe after having failed in national politics, Varoufakis has decided to form his own pan-European political movement.

The difficulty with this approach is best summed up by the debate between two German thinkers, Jürgen Habermas and Wolfgang Streeck.[7] Now in his late eighties, Habermas is probably Germany's most influential living intellectual. A philosopher who was already heavily involved in German political debates in the 1970s, he has gained an international reputation for his contribution to thinking about Europe's political future. Almost twenty years younger than Habermas, Wolfgang Streeck is a more recent arrival on the public intellectual scene. Trained as a sociologist, he spent much of his life studying the transformation of European labour markets and industrial relations. He was, until recently, director of one of Europe's most eminent social science institutions, the Max Planck Institute for the Study of Societies in Cologne. The Eurozone crisis has radicalized Streeck, turning him into one of the most vocal critics of contemporary capitalism.

Habermas's views have not changed. He has long believed that European integration needs to be political as well as economic. In order for the social gains won by Europe's welfare states to be preserved, the EU needs to integrate politically. A supranational democracy is the best way to defend Europe's high standards of living and its extensive regime of social rights. The logic of this position is clear, but Streeck criticizes Habermas for being naive and utopian. Streeck recommends we take Europe as it is and this Europe is more heterogeneous and more divided than ever. Differences between national societies are acute and there is no public appetite for the profound transformations of European politics that the creation of a supranational democracy would require. Streeck believes we should defend and strengthen national democracy, even if that means less Europe. One of Streeck's most well-known and controversial recommendations is to dismantle the Eurozone.[8] In addition to the fact that it is not working, it exerts too heavy a cost on national democratic decision-making. Habermas has accused Streeck of 'small-state nostalgia'. Streeck has replied that he is just being realistic and would rather be a realist than a utopian any day.

Politics begins at home

How to resolve this conflict between the European Union and national democracy? As this book has made clear, European integration has had a dramatic impact on the lives of citizens in Europe, but we cannot say that it has effaced the differences between national societies. In some ways, it has magnified these differences. The Eurozone has done this by removing key policy instruments from the hands of governments. Unable to vary the value of its currency, a country's economic future is shaped more than ever before by the structure of its society, its labour market traditions, the role and power of its middle class and the balance between savings and investment. Even the single market itself has not eliminated national barriers in Europe and, as we saw in Chapter 3, there is no single European economy.

We have also seen that European integration has coincided with important changes in the way societies in Europe are governed. A horizontal space has opened up, where national executives and officials cooperate intensively with each other across borders. This cooperation is overseen and facilitated by European institutions. Close ties of personal friendship and loyalty are created between politicians who face common problems and rely on each other for solutions. This sphere has become cut off from the everyday world of citizens in EU member states, where there is much less by way of connections that cross borders. Indeed, there are no European citizens as such, only national citizens whose status as an EU citizen comes from their belonging to an EU member state. What unites the populations of Europe is their hostility to their own political class and a deeply felt scepticism about politics. But this is no basis for common political action at the European level and many of the protests and political events that we have seen in Europe in recent years – as we saw in Chapter 4 – remain oriented around national questions.

Faced with continued social and economic heterogeneity

in Europe, and with a governing class accustomed to doing business together at the EU level, it is very difficult to see where any leap into a supranational democratic Europe would come from. Who would lead the charge? It is fanciful to believe that out of the present-day European Union chrysalis, organized under the guise of secrecy and run by national political elites, will emerge a beautiful, supranational and democratic European butterfly. Those who see in our current leaders agents of a new European-wide democracy are the real utopians.

If we want to reconcile Europe with democracy, we should return to what actually exists in Europe – a multitude of national democracies. Does this mean returning to the pristine and untouched version of national democracy that some critics of the EU dream about? They suggest that national democracy would be alive and well if only we were able to push back the tide of European integration. The EU, from this perspective, is a force choking democracy on the continent.

This view is as misguided as those wishing for a supranational European democracy. We have seen in this book that Europe is no longer composed of nation-states, defined by a clear sense of national belonging. Nation-states in the traditional sense rested upon a relationship between the state and its people, summed up emotionally and politically in the idea of the nation – a body of citizens, engaged together in forging their political destiny. Citizens often did not agree on what that destiny should be, and these disagreements were the basis for national party systems and struggles between left and right. Identification with one's nation did battle with loyalty to a political party or to a social class. Nevertheless, the relationship between state and society was strong and based around a clear logic of representation.

Europe is today a continent of member states. While national political elites increasingly rely on EU membership as a basis for their own authority, citizens have lost faith in their own governments. Identification with a political party has declined dramatically across the continent. Parties are often the institution of public and political life which people trust the least. In a Europe of member states, governments rely on each other for their authority while citizens search for legitimacy outside politics altogether. Legitimacy comes either from expertise, from knowledge, in the form of technocracy, or it comes from 'the people', a term that is used not as a metaphor for politics but as an alternative to the grubby political world of parties, interests and elites. Political competition is increasingly structured around these two poles of populism and technocracy. This is the real world of national democracy in Europe. Political life has been hollowed out of many of its traditional conflicts and debates. Parties of the left and the right seek to redefine themselves in terms of expertise and an appeal to 'the people' as a whole. There is little confidence in the ability of national governments to shape society and there are few ideas anyway about what that would mean even if governments did claim to have that power.

The real challenge for citizens in Europe is to give their own national political life a sense of purpose again: to see politics as a space where collective destinies can and will be shaped. 'Ever close union', as it is practised today, will not achieve this. It will only widen the gap between national elites and their own populations. Dismantling the EU would not by itself reinvigorate national democratic life. However, it would help us see that the problems of democracy in Europe do not originate in the EU but in the changing relations between states and their citizens at the national level. All of this does not mean abandoning the idea of Europe. It means recasting Europe as a new project of internationalism rather than as a tired one of integration or federalism. The main lesson to take from this 'Citizen's Guide' is that once you have properly understood what the EU is and what it does, you will see that the real challenges ahead do not lie in Brussels. They lie where you are, wherever in Europe that may be.

Notes

INTRODUCTION: SOLVING THE EU RIDDLE

1   Paul Magnette, *What is the European Union? Nature and Prospects* (Basingstoke: Palgrave Macmillan, 2005); J. H. H. Weiler, *The Constitution of Europe: "Do the New Clothes have an Emperor?" and Other Essays on European Integration* (Cambridge: Cambridge University Press, 1999).
2   John Laughland, *The Tainted Source: The Undemocratic Origins of the European Idea* (London: Little, Brown, 1997); Bill Cash, *Against a Federal Europe: The Battle for Britain* (London: Duckworth, 1991).
3   Will Dahlgreen, 'EU referendum: would no really mean no?', YouGov, 20 August 2015.
4   For more on this idea of member statehood, see Christopher J. Bickerton, *European Integration: From Nation States to Member States* (Oxford: Oxford University Press, 2012).

CHAPTER 1: WHO RULES EUROPE?

1   Martin Sandbu, *Europe's Orphan: The Future of the Euro and the Politics of Debt* (Oxford: Princeton University Press, 2015), p. 132.
2   Nereo Peñalver García and Julian Priestley, *The Making of a European President* (Basingstoke: Palgrave Macmillan, 2015), p. xii.
3   Ian Parker, 'The Greek Warrior', *The New Yorker*, 3 August 2015.
4   Henry Foy, 'Lunch with the FT: Donald Tusk', *Financial Times*, 28 November 2014.
5   Anne-Sylvaine Chassany, Alex Barker and Duncan Robinson, 'Greece Talks: "Sorry, but there is no way you are leaving this room"', *Financial Times*, 13 July 2015.

6   Strictly speaking, there are 18,857 full-time staff members of the European Commission. To that number we usually add bodies formally attached to the European Commission, such as the Joint Research Centre and the Anti-Fraud Office, OLAF. Adding those brings the number up to just under 25,000. Figures are taken from the Draft General Budget of the European Union for 2016, Section III Commission, p. 1554.

7   Bruno Waterfield, '10,000 European officials better paid than David Cameron', *Daily Telegraph*, 21 May 2014.

8   In 2013 the European Commission President José Manuel Barroso earned 304,221 euros, on top of which we must add residential and entertainment allowances. The French president earned 170,280 euros in the same year. The Spanish prime minister was paid 78,000 euros a year. The figures are taken from Roger Bootle, *The Trouble With Europe*, 2nd edn (London: Nicholas Brealey, 2015), p. 97.

9   This phrase was used in a speech Angela Merkel gave at the College of Europe in Bruges, 2 November 2010.

10 García and Priestley, *The Making of a European President*, p. 15.

11 For an overview of the Commission since 1992, see John Peterson, 'The Commission and the New Intergovernmentalism: Calm within the Storm?', in Christopher Bickerton, Dermot Hodson and Uwe Puetter (eds), *The New Intergovernmentalism: States and Supranational Actors in the Post-Maastricht Era* (Oxford: Oxford University Press, 2015).

12 A point made by a former EU Commission official in discussion with the author, December 2015.

13 The phrase comes from Merkel's 2010 speech in Bruges (see note 9).

14 Most terms such as this are taken from the French. Like *acquis communautaire*, a term referring to the body of the EU's laws, which states applying to join the EU have to show they have translated into domestic law.

15 Hermann Schmitt, Sara B. Hobolt and Sebastian Adrian Popa, '"Spitzenkandidaten" in the 2014 European Parliament Election: Does Campaign Personalization Increase the Propensity to Turn Out?', unpublished paper, European Consortium for Political Research conference, Glasgow, September 2014.

16 Charlemagne, 'Stop the Music', *The Economist*, 9 January 2016.

17 Interview with the *Financial Times*, 22 December 2015.

18 The full title of the report is *The Five Presidents' Report: Completing Europe's Economic and Monetary Union*. Available at: https://ec.europa.eu/priorities/publications/five-presidents-report-completing-europes-economic-and-monetary-union_en

19   Helen Wallace, William Wallace and Carole Webb (eds), *Policy-Making in the European Communities* (Oxford: Wiley, 1977), p. 21.

20   Simon Hix and Sara Hagemann, 'Does the UK win or lose in the Council of Ministers?', LSE European Politics and Policy blog, 11 February 2015.

21   This is according to Yanis Varoufakis's description of Eurogroup meetings: 'All eyes are on [Schäuble], and what he is going to say, and the tone in which he's going to say it.' Cited in Parker, 'The Greek Warrior', p. 53.

22   George Packer, 'The Quiet German', *The New Yorker*, 1 December 2014.

23   Packer, 'The Quiet German'.

24   Packer, 'The Quiet German'.

25   For a more extended discussion of this trend of weakening supranational institutions and the creation of new agencies, see Christopher J. Bickerton, Dermot Hodson and Uwe Puetter, 'The New Intergovernmentalism: European Integration in the Post-Maastricht Era', *Journal of Common Market Studies*, 53(4), 2015, pp. 703–22.

26   Christopher Bickerton and Bruno Waterfield, *No Means No! Essays on the Eve of the European Council Meeting* (London: Manifesto Club, 4 December 2008), pp. 6–7.

27   Deirdre Curtin, 'Top Secret Europe', Inaugural lecture at the University of Amsterdam, October 2011, p. 16.

28   Perry Anderson, *The New Old World* (London: Verso, 2009), p. 62.

29   Edoardo Bressanelli, Adrienne Héritier, Christel Koop and Christine Reh, 'The Informal Politics of Co-decision: Introducing a New Data Set on Early Agreements in the European Union', *EUI Working Paper* 2014/64.

CHAPTER 2: WHERE DID THE EUROPEAN UNION COME FROM?

1   Peter Gowan and Perry Anderson (eds), *The Question of Europe* (London: Verso, 1997), p. 92.

2   Tony Judt, *A Grand Illusion? An Essay on Europe* (New York: New York University Press, 2011 [1996]), p. 133.

3   Norman Davies, *Heart of Europe: The Past in Poland's Present* (1984; new edn, Oxford: Oxford University Press, 2001), p. 71.

4   Konrad H. Jarausch, *Out of Ashes: A New History of Europe in the Twentieth Century* (Oxford: Princeton University Press, 2015), p. 423.

5   Jarausch, *Out of Ashes*, p. 414. Leopold's conduct during the war had turned opinion against him and after an unstable few years (Belgium went through

nine governments between 1945 and 1950) Leopold was forced to abdicate in favour of his son, the twenty-year-old Boudewijn.

6   Paul Arblaster, *A History of the Low Countries*, 2nd edn (Basingstoke: Palgrave Macmillan, 2012), p. 236.

7   Friedrich A. Hayek, *The Road to Serfdom* (London: Routledge and Kegan Paul, 1944), p. 3. Hayek's book was dedicated to 'the socialists of all parties'.

8   James Sheehan calls these 'civilian states'. See his book *Where Have All the Soldiers Gone? The Transformation of Modern Europe* (Boston: Houghton Mifflin, 2008).

9   Sven Steinmo, *The Evolution of Modern States: Sweden, Japan and the United States* (Cambridge: Cambridge University Press, 2010), pp. 54–5.

10 Andrew Shonfield, *Modern Capitalism: The Changing Balance of Public and Private Power* (Oxford: Oxford University Press, 1965), p. 126.

11 Under the terms of the Treaty of Paris of 1951, which created the Coal and Steel Community, the Community was given a lifespan of only fifty years. As planned, it 'disappeared' on 23 July 2002. For the detail, see Fiona Hayes-Renshaw and Helen Wallace, *The Council of Ministers*, 2nd edn (Basingstoke: Palgrave Macmillan, 2006), p. 7.

12 Richard Vinen, *A History in Fragments: Europe in the Twentieth Century* (London: Little, Brown, 2000), p. 354.

13 Nicholas Crafts, 'Fifty Years of Economic Growth in Western Europe: No Longer Catching Up But Falling Behind?', Stanford Institute for Economic Policy and Research Discussion Paper No. 03-21, 10 November 2003.

14 For the best treatment of this, see Ann-Christina Knudsen, *Farmers on Welfare: The Making of Europe's Common Agricultural Policy* (Ithaca, New York: Cornell University Press, 2009).

15 Paul-Henri Spaak, *The Continuing Battle: Memoirs of a European, 1936–1966* (London: Weidenfeld and Nicolson, 1971), p. 230.

16 Gert Oostindie and Inge Klinkers, *Decolonising the Caribbean: Dutch Policies in a Comparative Perspective* (Amsterdam: Amsterdam University Press, 2003), p. 69.

17 Report by Leo Tindemans, Prime Minister of Belgium to the European Council, 1975, p. 11.

18 Paul Ginsborg, *A History of Contemporary Italy: Society and Politics 1943–1988* (London: Penguin, 1990), p. 298.

19 Michael Loriaux, *France after Hegemony: International Change and Financial Reform* (Ithaca, New York: Cornell University Press, 1991), p. 201.

20 Ginsborg, *History of Contemporary Italy*, p. 407.

21 Eric Hobsbawm, *Age of Extremes: The Short Twentieth Century 1914–1991* (London: Michael Joseph, 1994), p. 483.

22 Mary Elise Sarotte, *1989: The Struggle to Create Post-Cold War Europe* (Oxford: Princeton University Press, 2011).

23 John Peterson, 'The Commission and the New Intergovernmentalism: Calm within the Storm?', in Christopher Bickerton, Dermot Hodson and Uwe Puetter (eds), *The New Intergovernmentalism: States and Supranational Actors in the Post-Maastricht Era* (Oxford: Oxford University Press, 2015), p. 188.

24 Alan Milward, 'The Social Bases of Monetary Union?' in Gowan and Anderson (eds), *The Question of Europe*, pp. 156–60.

25 OECD data from the OECD website's data archive.

CHAPTER 3: IS THE EUROPEAN UNION A CAPITALIST CLUB?

1   Pierre Lascoumes and Patrick Le Galès (eds), *Gouverner par les instruments* (Paris: Presse de Sciences Po, 2004).

2   For this account of Balassa, see André Sapir, 'European Integration at the Crossroads: A Review Essay on the 50th Anniversary of Bela Balassa's *Theory of Economic Integration*', *Journal of Economic Literature*, 49(4), 2011, pp. 1200–229.

3   This was replaced in 2014 by the Eurasian Economic Union, which is one step along on Balassa's list of stages in economic integration.

4   Richard Mayne, *The Recovery of Europe: From Devastation to Unity* (London: Weidenfeld and Nicolson, 1970), p. 118.

5   A detailed account of the ECSC is given in Chapter 2.

6   Alasdair R. Young, 'The Single Market: Deregulation, Reregulation, and Integration', in Helen Wallace, Mark A. Pollack and Alasdair R. Young (eds), *Policy-Making in the European Union* (Oxford: Oxford University Press, 2010), p. 110.

7   Young, 'The Single Market: Deregulation, Reregulation, and Integration', p. 110.

8   Fritz Scharpf, *Governing in Europe: Effective and Democratic?* (Oxford: Oxford University Press, 1999), p. 54.

9   Anand Menon, *Europe: The State of the Union* (London: Atlantic, 2008), p. 154.

10 *Europe 2020: A European Strategy for Smart, Sustainable and Inclusive Growth*, Brussels: Communication from the Commission, COM(March 2010) final.

11   'The Big Read: Bank Rescues', *Financial Times*, 5 January 2016.

12   Hugo Dixon, 'Europe is a market not a superstate', *Financial Times*, 17/18 October 2015.

13   See the opening of Daniel Mügge's excellent book which takes Smith's phrase as its title. Daniel Mügge, *Widen the Market, Narrow the Competition: Banker Interests and the Making of an European Capital Market* (Colchester: ECPR Press, 2010). The quote is from Adam Smith, *The Wealth of Nations*, Chapter 11, first published in 1779.

14   For a nice explanation of this, see Chapter 12 of Ha-Joon Chang, *Economics: The User's Guide* (London: Penguin, 2014).

15   Willem Molle, *The Economics of European Integration: Theory, Practice, Policy* (Aldershot: Ashgate, 2001), p. 115.

16   Stefan Houpt, Pedro Lains and Lennart Schön, 'Sectoral developments, 1945–2000', in Stephen Broadberry and Kevin H. O'Rourke (eds), *The Cambridge Economic History of Modern Europe*, Volume 2: *1870 to the Present* (Cambridge: Cambridge University Press, 2010), p. 349.

17   On this section, see Molle, *The Economics of European Integration*, Chapter 8.

18   Mügge, *Widen the Market, Narrow the Competition*, p. 47.

19   Mügge, *Widen the Market, Narrow the Competition*, p. 41.

20   Mügge, *Widen the Market, Narrow the Competition*, p. 36.

21   This is a bit like the National Insurance number in the UK, or the Carte Vitale in France.

22   Jonathan Portes, 'Labour Mobility in the European Union', in Steven N. Durlauf and Lawrence E. Blume (eds), *The New Palgrave Dictionary of Economics*, 2nd edn (Basingstoke: Palgrave Macmillan, 2015).

23   Portes, 'Labour Mobility in the European Union'.

24   Office for National Statistics, *Population by Country of Birth and Nationality Report: August 2015* (London, 2015).

25   Portes, 'Labour Mobility in the European Union'.

26   Portes, 'Labour Mobility in the European Union'.

27   Portes, 'Labour Mobility in the European Union'.

28   Stephen Gill, 'European Governance and New Constitutionalism: Economic and Monetary Union and Alternatives to disciplinary neoliberalism in Europe', *New Political Economy*, 3(1), 1998, pp. 5–26.

29   The classical academic article defending the use of policy rules against the exercise of political discretion was by Finn Kydland and Edward Prescott in 1977, 'Rules rather than discretion: The inconsistency of optimal plans', *The Journal of Political Economy*, 85(3), June 1977, pp. 473–92. For a discussion of fiscal rules, see Barry Eichengreen, Robert Feldman, Jeffrey Liebman,

Jürgen von Hagen and Charles Wyplosz, *Public Debts: Buts, Bolts and Worries: Geneva Report on the World Economy* 13 (Geneva: ICMB/CEPR, September 2011). For a critical discussion of the implications of this approach for European democracy, see the chapters in Armin Schäfer and Wolfgang Streeck (eds), *Politics in the Age of Austerity* (Cambridge: Polity, 2013).

30 Vivien A. Schmidt, 'Forgotten Democratic Legitimacy: "Governing by the Rules" and "Ruling by the numbers"', in M. Matthijs and M. Blyth (eds), *The Future of the Euro* (New York: Oxford University Press, 2015).

31 Young, 'The Single Market: Deregulation, Reregulation, and Integration', p. 123.

32 Young, 'The Single Market: Deregulation, Reregulation, and Integration', p. 122.

33 Houpt et al., 'Sectoral developments, 1945–2000', p. 357. The figure is taken from the OECD's database.

34 Young, 'The Single Market: Deregulation, Reregulation, and Integration', p. 123.

35 This is the *Laval* vs *Svenska Byggnadsarbetareförbundet* case of 2007. This account draws on A. C. L. Davies, 'One Step Forward, Two Steps Back? The Viking and Laval Cases in the ECJ', *Industrial Law Journal*, 37(2), 2008, pp. 126–48.

36 Helen Warrell, 'UK Migration: Toil, trouble and tension', *Financial Times*, 13 August 2015.

37 Young, 'The Single Market: Deregulation, Reregulation, and Integration', p. 124.

38 James Heartfield, 'State capitalism in Britain', *Mute Magazine*, 24 June 2009; available at http://www.metamute.org/editorial/articles/state-capitalism-britain.

39 John Plender, 'Policy backdrop is favourable for pick-up in Eurozone growth', *Financial Times*, 6 January 2016.

40 This section draws on Nathaniel Copsey, *Rethinking the European Union* (Basingstoke: Palgrave Macmillan, 2015), especially Chapter 4.

41 The British Queen received in 2008 well over half a million euros in EU subsidies. In the same year, the Duke of Marlborough, who lives in the baroque palace of Blenheim in Oxfordshire, received between 1 and 1.5 million euros of subsidies. The Duke of Westminster, the ninth richest person in the UK in 2015 with a fortune of over £8 billion, received a similar amount from the EU. Copsey, *Rethinking the European Union*, p. 108.

42 Tony Judt, *A Grand Illusion? An Essay on Europe* (New York: New York University Press, 2011 [1996]), p. 528.

43 Copsey, *Rethinking the European Union*, p. 110.

44 Copsey, *Rethinking the European Union*, p. 115. The data Copsey refers to are from Kaja Bonesmo Fredriksen, 'Income inequality in the European Union', OECD Economics Department Working Paper, No. 952, April 2012.

45 Gøsta Esping-Andersen, *The Three Worlds of Welfare Capitalism* (Cambridge: Polity Press, 1990).

46 Colin Crouch, 'Privatized Keynesianism: An Unacknowledged Policy Regime', *British Journal of International Relations*, 11(3), 2009, pp. 382–99.

CHAPTER 4: WHO IS AGAINST EUROPE?

1 Peter Mair, 'Political Opposition and the European Union', *Government and Opposition*, 42(1), Winter 2007, pp. 1–17.

2 In Mair's words, in the EU 'we emphatically lack the right to organize opposition . . . We lack the capacity to do so, and, above all, we lack an arena in which to do so', in 'Political Opposition and the European Union', p. 7.

3 Speech by Donald Tusk to the Dutch Liberal Party (VVD) in the Hague, 24 October 2015.

4 Matteo Renzi, 'Europe isn't working for this generation', *The Guardian*, 21 January 2016.

5 Giulia Segreti and Guy Dinmore, 'EU like "an old boring aunt" lecturing Italy, says Renzi', *Financial Times*, 26 June 2014.

6 The phrase 'permissive consensus' was originally coined by Valdimer O. Key Jr in his 1961 book *Public Opinion and American Democracy* (New York: Knopf). It was taken up and applied to Western Europe by L. N. Lindberg and S. A. Scheingold in their influential 1970 book *Europe's Would-Be Polity* (Englewood Cliffs, New Jersey: Prentice Hall).

7 For a very useful discussion of the French Communist Party's views on European integration, see Emile-François Callot, 'The French Communist Party and Europe: the idea and its implementation (1945–1985)', *European Journal of Political Research*, 16(3), May 1988, pp. 301–16.

8 Callot, 'The French Communist Party and Europe: the idea and its implementation (1945–1985)', p. 302.

9   Maud Bracke, 'From the Atlantic to the Urals? Italian and French communism and the question of Europe, 1956–73', *Journal of European Integration History*, 14(2), 2007, pp. 33–53.

10 Callot, 'The French Communist Party and Europe: the idea and its implementation (1945–1985)', p. 311.

11 Cited in Hugo Young, *This Blessed Plot: Britain and Europe from Churchill to Blair* (London: Macmillan, 1998), p. 151.

12 John Lahr (ed.), *The Diaries of Kenneth Tynan* (London: Bloomsbury, 2001), p. 248.

13 Hugo Young, *This Blessed Plot*, p. 378.

14 Ian Buruma, *Murder in Amsterdam: The Death of Theo Van Gogh and the Limits of Tolerance* (London: Atlantic Books, 2006), p. 50.

15 Tom Mueller, 'Beppe's Inferno', *The New Yorker*, 4 February 2008.

16 The term comes from a bestselling book in Italy, called *La Casta*, written by Gian Antonio Stella and Sergio Rizzo, published in 2007. This term has been taken up by a number of other well-known figures, such as the leader of Podemos in Spain, Pablo Iglesias.

17 By 2008, Grillo's blog was reported to be the eighth most read in the world (Mueller, 'Beppe's Inferno', p. 2).

18 Beppe Grillo, interview with BBC, 13 November 2014.

19 Grillo and Casaleggio, cited in Simone Natale and Andrea Ballatore, 'The web will kill them all: new media, digital utopia, and political struggle in the Italian 5-Star Movement', *Media, Culture and Society*, 36(1), January 2014, pp. 105–21, p. 114.

20 Hugo Young, *This Blessed Plot*, p. 409. Young recounts that Goldsmith made this declaration from his private booth in the London restaurant Wilton's, which is tucked in next to all the high-end tailors on Jermyn Street, off Piccadilly.

21 This is best documented in the excellent book by Matthew Goodwin and Robert Ford, *Revolt on the Right: Explaining Support for the Radical Right in Britain* (London: Routledge, 2014).

22 Carlo Invernizzi Accetti and Chris Bickerton, 'Neither Left nor Right in France: How the National Front Has Changed Politics', *Foreign Affairs*, 18 February 2016.

23 Wolfgang Streeck, 'The SPD under Merkel', *The Current Moment*, 2 June 2014.

24 Mary Kaldor, Sabine Selchow, Sean Deel and Tamsin Murray-Leach, *The 'Bubbling Up' of Subterranean Politics in Europe*, Report for the Civil Society and Human Security Research Unit, London School of Economics, 2012.

25 Kaldor et al., *The 'Bubbling Up' of Subterranean Politics in Europe*.

26 For an extended account of this, see 'National Horizons to Europe's Crisis', *The Current Moment*, 16 November 2011.

27 Gideon Rachman, 'EU leaders cannot simply ignore the populist howl', *Financial Times*, 26 May 2014.

CHAPTER 5: WILL THE EU KEEP ON EXPANDING?

1 In full, article 2 says that 'The Union is founded on the values of respect for human dignity, freedom, democracy, equality, the rule of law and respect for human rights, including the rights of persons belonging to minorities. These values are common to the Member States in a society in which pluralism, non-discrimination, tolerance, justice, solidarity and equality between women and men prevail.'

2 *The Balkans in Europe's Future*, Report of the International Commission on the Balkans (Sofia: April 2005), p. 28.

3 The comment was made by Günter Verheugen, Commissioner for enlargement from 1999 to 2004 under the Presidency of Romano Prodi.

4 Robert Kagan, *Paradise and Power: America and Europe in the New World Order* (London: Atlantic, 2003), p. 3.

5 Mark Leonard, 'EU ain't seen nothin' yet', *New Humanist*, March/April 2005, p. 26.

6 The French journalist Michel Meyer has documented this after accessing recently opened archives. His 2009 book in French is *Histoire secrète de la chute du mur de Berlin* [A Secret History of the Fall of the Berlin Wall] (Paris: Odile Jacob). For a more general argument about the collapse of the existing elite in 1989, see Stephen Kotkin, *Uncivil Society: 1989 and the Implosion of the Communist Establishment* (New York: The Modern Library, 2009). This argument was made much earlier by Tony Judt in his famous 1988 article 'The Dilemmas of Dissidence: The Politics of Opposition in East-central Europe'.

7 Jacques Rupnik, 'In Search of a New Model', *Journal of Democracy*, 21(1), January 2010, pp. 105–12, p. 106.

8 Similar results are found in other Eastern European countries. For instance, a March poll in 2009 in Germany found that a majority of those who had lived in East Germany thought that life was better in the GDR. See Rupnik, 'In Search of a New Model', p. 106.

9   Alan Renwick, 'What happens if we vote for Brexit?', *The Constitution Unit*, 19 January 2016.

10 The Norwegians voted on EU membership again in 1994, and rejected it a second time.

11 Cited in Stephen Wall, *A Stranger in Europe: Britain and the EU from Thatcher to Blair* (Oxford: Oxford University Press, 2008), p. 2.

12 Alan Milward, *Official History of the United Kingdom and the European Community*, Volume 1: *The Rise and Fall of a National Strategy* (London: Routledge, 2002).

13 Wall, *A Stranger in Europe*, p. 4.

14 Dominic Webb and Matthew Keep, 'In Brief: UK–EU economic relations', House of Commons Library, Briefing paper 06091, 19 January 2016.

15 Tony Judt, *Postwar: A History of Europe Since 1945* (London: Heinemann, 2005), p. 517.

16 Judt, *Postwar*, p. 507.

17 Judt, *Postwar*, p. 522.

18 Barry Eichengreen and Andrea Boltho, 'The economic impact of European integration', in Stephen Broadberry and Kevin H. O'Rourke (eds), *The Cambridge Economic History of Modern Europe*, Volume 2: *1870 to the Present* (Cambridge: Cambridge University Press, 2010), p. 271.

19 Massimo La Torre and Agustín José Menéndez , '¿Cavacada o golpe de estado a la europea?', *InfoLibre*, 30 October 2015; available at http://www.infolibre.es/noticias/luces_rojas/2015/10/26/cavacada_golpe_estado_europea_39638_1121.html.

20 Peter Wise, 'Left-wing alliance poised to take power in Portugal', *Financial Times*, 9 November 2015.

21 Quoted on p. 430 of Norman Davies's book *Heart of Europe: The Past in Poland's Present* (1984; new edn, Oxford: Oxford University Press, 2001).

22 Those EU member states who have not yet joined the euro, but are committed to doing so, are called 'member states with a derogation', meaning EU member states that have not yet fulfilled the necessary conditions for the adoption of the euro. Slovenia was the first to join, in 2007. Malta and Cyprus joined in 2008. Then it was Slovakia in 2009, Estonia in 2011, Latvia in 2014 and Lithuania in 2015.

23 See the account in Christian Lequesne's *La France dans la Nouvelle Europe: Assumer le changement d'échelle* (Paris: Les Presses de Sciences Po, 2007).

24 Perry Anderson, *The New Old World* (London: Verso, 2009), p. 53.

25 Laurence Whitehead, *The International Dimensions of Democratization: Europe and the Americas*, expanded edn (Oxford: Oxford University Press, 2001), p. 415.

26 Vesselin Dimitrov, 'From Laggard to Pacesetter: Bulgaria's Road to EMU', in Kenneth Dyson (ed.), *Enlarging the Euro Area: External Empowerment and Domestic Transformation in East Central Europe* (Oxford: Oxford University Press, 2006), pp. 150–51.

27 Attila Agh, 'Europeanization of policy-making in East Central Europe: the Hungarian approach to EU accession', *Journal of European Public Policy*, 6(5), 1999, pp. 839–54.

28 Kristi Raik, 'EU Accession of Central and Eastern European Countries: Democracy and Integration as Conflicting Logics', *East European Politics and Societies*, 18(4), 2004, pp. 567–94.

29 James Hughes, Gwendolyn Sasse and Claire Gordon, 'Saying "maybe" to the return to Europe', *European Union Politics*, 3(3), 2002, pp. 327–55.

30 Ivan Krastev, 'The Strange Death of the Liberal Consensus', *Journal of Democracy*, 18(4), October 2007, pp. 56–63.

31 Anderson, *The New Old World*, p. 53.

32 Magnus Feldman, 'The Baltic States: Pacesetting on EMU Accession and the Consolidation of Domestic Stability Culture', in Dyson (ed.), *Enlarging the Euro Area*; Frank Bönker, 'From Pacesetter to Laggard: The Political Economy of Negotiating Fit in the Czech Republic', in Dyson (ed.), *Enlarging the Euro Area*; Béla Greskovits, 'The First Shall Be the Last? Hungary's Road to EMU', in Dyson (ed.), *Enlarging the Euro Area*; Julius Horvath, 'The May 1997 Currency Crisis in the Czech Republic', *Post-Communist Economies*, 11(3), 1999, pp. 277–98; 'Stressed out: The fight to avoid a sixth euro-zone bail-out reaches a climax', *The Economist*, 30 November 2013.

33 The most active banks in Eastern Europe have included Raiffeisen (Austria), Erste (Austria), KBC (Belgium) and Swedbank (Sweden).

34 Piroska Mohácsi Nagy, 'Financial Market Governance: Evolution and Convergence', in Dyson (ed.), *Enlarging the Euro Area*, p. 244.

35 European Bank for Reconstruction and Development, *Transition Report 2013: Stuck in Transition?* London, 2013.

36 Pieter Spiegel and Henry Foy, 'Poland crackdown on media and courts faces probe by Brussels', *Financial Times*, 5 January 2016.

37 David Ost, *The Defeat of Solidarity: Anger and Politics in Postcommunist Europe* (Ithaca, New York: Cornell University Press, 2005).

38   Chris J. Bickerton, 'From Brezhnev to Brussels: Transformations of sovereignty in Eastern Europe', *International Politics*, 46, 2009, p. 742.

39   Anderson, *The New Old World*, p. 53.

CHAPTER 6: COULD THE EU BECOME A SUPERPOWER?

1   Chris Patten, *Not Quite the Diplomat: Home Truths about World Affairs* (London: Allen Lane, 2005), p. 155.

2   Anand Menon, 'Divided and Declining? Europe in a Changing World', The JCMS Annual Review Lecture, *JCMS Annual Review of the European Union in 2013*, 52(S1), September 2014, pp. 5–24, at p. 20.

3   Orysia Lutsevych, 'Do not fail Ukraine in its battle for European values', *Financial Times*, 21 February 2014.

4   See his article in the *Financial Times* on 10 March 2014.

5   Ivan Krastev and Mark Leonard, 'Europe's Shattered Dream of Order', *Foreign Affairs*, May/June 2015, p. 49.

6   Patten, *Not Quite the Diplomat*, p. 152.

7   Transmitted on the *News at 10* in the UK. Cited in Mark Almond, *Europe's Backyard War: War in the Balkans* (London: Mandarin, 1994), p. 32.

8   Almond, *Europe's Backyard War*, p. 51.

9   Richard Youngs, *Europe's Decline and Fall: The Struggle Against Global Irrelevance* (London: Profile, 2010), p. 25.

10   Editorial, *Financial Times*, 24 February 2014.

11   Ellie Geranmayeh, 'Europe's Edge: By Engaging With Iran, Europe Can Assert Its Power', *Foreign Affairs*, 19 July 2015.

12   Patten, *Not Quite the Diplomat*, p. 150.

13   'Waiting for the big call', *The Economist*, 16 September 2010.

14   Jean Quatremer, 'Les Weekends de Lady Ashton', *Coulisses de Bruxelles* blog, 18 March 2010.

15   Ronald D. Asmus, *A Little War That Shook the World: Georgia, Russia and the Future of the West* (Basingstoke: Palgrave Macmillan, 2010), p. 203.

16   Nick Witney, 'How to stop the Demilitarization of Europe', *Policy Brief*, European Council of Foreign Relations, 2011.

17   Bruno Waterfield, 'Baroness Ashton will be paid £400,000 by the EU to do nothing', *Daily Telegraph*, 5 April 2013.

18   Case C-91/05, *Commission vs Council*, judgment delivered on 20 May 2008.

19   Judy Dempsey, 'Judy asks: Can Tusk boost EU foreign policy?', Carnegie Europe, 3 December 2014.

20   Thierry Tardy, *CSDP in action – What contribution to international security?* Chaillot Paper 134 (Paris: European Union Institute for Security Studies, May 2015).

21   A calculation made using European Union Institute for Security Studies figures for the missions. This number includes international and local staff.

22   Tardy, *CSDP in action – What contribution to international security?*, p. 23.

23   Tardy, *CSDP in action – What contribution to international security?*, p. 32.

24   Cited in Krastev and Leonard, 'Europe's Shattered Dream of Order', p. 49.

25   Klaus Lorres, 'The United States and the "Demilitarization" of Europe: Myth or Reality?', *Politique Étrangère*, 1, Spring 2014.

26   Lorres, 'The United States and the "Demilitarization" of Europe: Myth or Reality?'.

27   Lorres, 'The United States and the "Demilitarization" of Europe: Myth or Reality?'.

28   James Sheehan, *Where Have All the Soldiers Gone? The Transformation of Modern Europe* (Boston: Houghton Mifflin, 2008), p. 176.

29   'Fighter jet sales drive French military exports', *Financial Times*, 20 January 2016.

30   'Military Spending in Europe in the Wake of the Ukraine Crisis', Media Background, 15 April (Stockholm: Stockholm International Peace Research Institute, 2015).

31   Sheehan, *Where Have All the Soldiers Gone?*, p. 178.

32   François Duchêne, *Jean Monnet: The First Statesman of Interdependence* (London: W. W. Norton and Co., 1994).

33   Sheehan, *Where Have All the Soldiers Gone?*, p. 165.

34   For a full treatment of this 'late development' of nationalism as a political ideology, see Eric Hobsbawm *Nations and Nationalism since 1780* (Cambridge: Cambridge University Press, 1990). For an excellent and brief typology of different nationalisms, see Perry Anderson, 'Internationalism: A Breviary', *New Left Review*, 14, 2002.

35   David Leakey, 'ESDP and Civil/Military Cooperation: Bosnia and Herzegovina', in Anne Deighton and Victor Mauer (eds), *Securing Europe? Implementing the European Security Strategy* (Zurich: Centre for Security Studies, 2006), p. 59.

36   Parag Khanna, 'The Metrosexual Superpower', *Foreign Policy*, 27 October 2009.

37 Javier Solana, Speech at the Annual Conference of the European Union
    Institute for Security Studies, in EUISS (ed.), *EU Security and Defence: Core
    Documents 2005* (Paris: EUISS, 2006).

38 Standard Eurobarometer, 84, Autumn 2015, *First Results*, p. 13.

39 Jürgen Habermas, *Europe: A Faltering Project* (Cambridge: Polity Press,
    2009), p. 57.

CONCLUSION: THE EU VERSUS DEMOCRACY

1   When asked why he was President, Varoufakis would reply that Greeks in
    the 1970s were 'the blacks of Europe'. See Ian Parker, 'The Greek Warrior',
    The New Yorker, 3 August 2015.

2   Parker, 'The Greek Warrior', p. 52.

3   See the explanation of the Eurogroup and Protocol 14 on the European
    Union's website: http://eur-lex.europa.eu/legal-content/EN/TXT/PDF/?uri
    =OJ:C:2007:306:FULL&from=EN#page=154.

4   Jan-Werner Müller, 'Rule-breaking', *London Review of Books*, 27 August
    2015, p. 3.

5   Claus Offe, *Europe Entrapped* (Cambridge: Polity, 2015), p. 3.

6   Giandomenico Majone, *Dilemmas of European Integration: The Ambiguities
    and Pitfalls of Integration by Stealth* (Oxford: Oxford University Press, 2005).

7   Streeck states his case in his 2014 book *Buying Time: The Delayed Crisis of
    Democratic Capitalism*, published by Verso. Habermas' review of Streeck's
    book is published as chapter 7 of his 2015 book *The Lure of Technocracy*,
    published by Polity Press. Streeck's response to Habermas is published in
    Wolfgang Streeck, 'Small-state nostalgia? The Currency Union, Germany and
    Europe: A Reply to Jürgen Habermas', *Constellations*, 21(2), 2014, pp. 213–21.

8   Wolfgang Streeck, 'L'Europe doit abandonner l'Euro [Europe must abandon
    the Euro]', *Le Monde*, 2 March 2015. See also Wolfgang Streeck, 'Brutish,
    nasty – and not even short: the ominous future of the eurozone', *The
    Guardian*, 17 August 2015.

Glossary

accession – the process through which countries wanting to join the EU have to pass, involving detailed negotiations with the European Commission and the adopting of all the EU's laws.

acquis communautaire – a French term referring to the body of EU law.

austerity – the term used to describe policies of cutting government spending implemented widely in the wake of the economic and financial crisis of 2008 and the increase in government budget deficits after bailing out banks.

Community Method – a technical term referring to a process of decision-making that involves the European Commission initiating legislative ideas and the Council and the European Parliament having co-decision powers; this approach has traditionally involved seeing the European Commission as the defender of the 'European interest' against the national interests of EU member states.

customs union – the creation of a trading bloc where all members have the same external tariff vis-à-vis non-members.

enlargement – the process whereby new countries join the EU.

Europe *à la carte* – a French term, meaning an approach to European integration in which countries move at different paces and can choose whether they want to cooperate more closely in certain policy areas or not; it literally means picking and choosing from a menu the areas in which countries can opt for closer cooperation or more integration.

European Communities – those bodies created by the two Treaties signed in 1957: the European Economic Community (EEC) and the European Atomic Energy Community (Euratom); the term also refers to the European Coal and Steel Community established in 1952.

Eurozone – the term used to refer to the single unit made up by all countries that use the euro, whose finance ministers sit on the Eurogroup and whose national central banks form the Eurosystem. The Eurozone's members are Austria, Cyprus, Belgium, Estonia, Finland, France, Germany, Greece, Ireland, Italy, Latvia, Lithuania, Luxembourg, Malta, the Netherlands, Portugal, Slovakia, Slovenia and Spain. Four micro-states (Andorra, Monaco, San Marino and Vatican City) also use the euro and have a formal arrangement with the EU, but they are not official members of the Eurozone. Montenegro and Kosovo have unilaterally adopted the euro as their currency, but are not Eurozone member states either.

federalism – an idea about the distribution of political power, usually in the form of a division between a 'federal' (i.e. centralized) and a state (i.e. regional) level; applied to the EU to mean the creation of a central European authority with some powers retained at the national level.

intergovernmentalism – an academic term referring to policy-making within the EU that remains within the hands of EU member states. Common policies are the result of negotiations between governments and power is retained by member states rather than delegated to institutions such as the European Commission or the European Central Bank. To describe a policy area as intergovernmental is not to refer to an absence of integration but rather a certain kind of European integration.

Keynesianism – a term used to describe a particular kind of economic policy that emphasizes the goals of full employment and uses government spending as a way of limiting the severity of economic downturns.

Maastricht Treaty – the treaty signed by twelve countries (Belgium, France, Germany, the Netherlands, Luxembourg, Italy, Spain, Portugal, Greece, United Kingdom, Denmark, Ireland) in the southern Dutch city of Maastricht in 1992 that committed its signatories (excluding the UK and Denmark who negotiated opt-outs) to creating a monetary union by 1999 and introduced a number of other important changes to European integration.

mutual recognition – a commitment to accept the regulatory standards of another country as being as good as those of the home country, for purposes of the exchange of goods and services.

neoliberalism – an economic or political concept that advocates a shift towards the embrace of free markets and competition. The term is often associated with the ideal of a small state, limited intervention, and low levels of taxation and government spending.

non-tariff barriers – barriers to trade that take a form other than that of customs duties on imports charged on the border.

Ordinary Legislative Procedure – the technical term, defined in the EU's treaties, which refers to the current way in which EU laws are made, involving co-decision between the Council of Ministers and the European Parliament.

pre-accession – a process of convergence with the laws and goals of the EU that takes place in advance of a country being formerly designated as a candidate state of the EU.

qualified majority voting – a decision-making procedure used in the Council of Ministers, whereby a decision is accepted if it has secured the votes of 55 per cent of member states that also represent at least 65 per cent of the total population of the EU.

rapporteur – a Member of the European Parliament (MEP) who is given the responsibility to draft a report on the activities of a parliamentary committee and represents that committee in the relevant negotiations with other EU institutions and with member states; committees usually select 'shadow rapporteurs' to accompany the lead rapporteur.

Schengen – a general term used to refer to the abolition of internal borders, leading to free movement of people within the EU. The original agreement was signed in the Luxembourg town of Schengen in 1985 by five member states: France, Germany, Belgium, the Netherlands and Luxembourg, and was focused on abolishing border checkpoints between these countries. More countries adhered to the Schengen Convention of 1990, but the UK and Ireland have never signed up to it.

single market – the term used to refer to the aspiration to have the completely free movement of people, capital, goods and services within the territory of the EU.

Spitzenkandidat – a German word meaning 'top candidate' that refers to the process of determining the President of the European Commission by tying the job to the outcome of the European Parliamentary elections; this process was first used in 2014.

supranationalism – an academic term used to describe a particular kind of policy-making at the EU level by which the European Commission has the sole right of initiative and power is delegated to European institutions that are independent from member states; *supra* comes from the Latin term meaning 'above', and so the term literally refers to an institution or a policy-making process that is 'above' national governments in the EU.

treaty change – the process whereby EU member states come together and agree unanimously to change some aspect of the EU treaties; this usually occurs with the convening of a conference of national governments of all EU member states.

trilogues – meetings between representatives from the European Commission, the Council and the European Parliament that have as their aim the reaching of an agreement on a draft law; these meetings are not public.

Further Reading

The following list is not meant to be exhaustive. It is also not a standard reading list for students taking a course on the European Union. It is intended as a lively way into the topics covered in these chapters. The choices reflect my own interest in journalism, history, biographies, political diaries and other sorts of readings that in my experience give some life and colour to the European Union. Textbooks and standard readings on the EU are valuable for academic courses, but are often oriented towards specific scholarly debates. This section starts with some thematic suggestions and then gives chapter-by-chapter recommendations for further reading.

EUROPEAN HISTORY SINCE 1945

- Konrad H. Jarausch, *Out of Ashes: A New History of Europe in the Twentieth Century* (Oxford: Princeton University Press, 2015)
- Tony Judt, *Postwar: A History of Europe Since 1945* (London: Heinemann, 2005)
- Tony Judt, *A Grand Illusion? An Essay on Europe* (New York: New York University Press, 2011 [1996])
- Ian Kershaw, *To Hell and Back: Europe, 1914–1949* (London: Allen Lane, 2015)

HISTORIES OF EUROPEAN INTEGRATION

- Perry Anderson, *The New Old World* (London: Verso, 2009)
- John Gillingham, *European Integration 1950–2003: Superstate or New Market Economy?* (Cambridge: Cambridge University Press, 2003)
- Richard Mayne, *The Recovery of Europe: From Devastation to Unity* (London: Weidenfeld and Nicolson, 1970)
- Luuk van Middelaar, *The Passage to Europe: How a Continent Became a Union* (London: Yale University Press, 2013)
- Alan S. Milward, *The European Rescue of the Nation-State*, 2nd edn (London: Routledge, 2000)

BIOGRAPHIES, AUTOBIOGRAPHIES, DIARIES AND PROFILES

- Willy Brandt, *People and Politics: The Years 1960–1975* (London: Collins, 1978)
- John Campbell, *Roy Jenkins: A Well-Rounded Life* (London: Jonathan Cape, 2014)
- Charles Grant, *Delors : Inside the House that Jacques Built* (London: Nicholas Brealey Publishing, 1994)
- Nicholas Henderson, *Mandarin: The Diaries of Nicholas Henderson* (London: Weidenfeld and Nicolson, 1994; new paperback edn, London: Phoenix Press, 2000)
- Roy Jenkins, *European Diary 1977–1981* (London: Collins, 1989)
- Tom Mueller, 'Beppe's Inferno', *The New Yorker*, 4 February 2008
- George Packer, 'The Quiet German', *The New Yorker*, 1 December 2014
- Ian Parker, 'The Greek Warrior', *The New Yorker*, 3 August 2015
- Chris Patten, *Not Quite the Diplomat: Home Truths about World Affairs* (London: Allen Lane, 2005)
- Philip Short, *Mitterrand: A Study in Ambiguity* (London: Bodley Head, 2013)
- Paul-Henri Spaak, *The Continuing Battle: Memoirs of a European, 1936–1966* (London: Weidenfeld and Nicolson, 1971)

CHAPTER 1: WHO RULES EUROPE?

- Deirdre Curtin, 'Overseeing Secrets in the EU: A Democratic Perspective', *Journal of Common Market Studies*, 52(3), April 2014, pp. 684–700
- Derk-Jan Eppink, *Life of European Mandarin: Inside the Commission* (Tielt, Belgium: Lannoo, 2007)
- Nereo Peñalver García and Julian Priestley, *The Making of a European President* (Basingstoke: Palgrave Macmillan, 2015)

CHAPTER 2: WHERE DID THE EUROPEAN UNION COME FROM?

- Christopher J. Bickerton, *European Integration: From Nation States to Member States* (Oxford: Oxford University Press, 2012)
- Mary Elise Sarotte, *1989: The Struggle to Create Post-Cold War Europe* (Oxford: Princeton University Press, 2011)
- Brendan Simms, *Europe: The Struggle for Supremacy, 1453 to the Present* (London: Allen Lane, 2013)

CHAPTER 3: IS THE EUROPEAN UNION A CAPITALIST CLUB?

- Matthias Matthijs and Mark Blyth (eds), *The Future of the Euro* (Oxford: Oxford University Press, 2015)
- Martin Sandbu, *Europe's Orphan: The Future of the Euro and the Politics of Debt* (Oxford: Princeton University Press, 2015)
- Fritz Scharpf, *Governing in Europe: Effective and Democratic?* (Oxford: Oxford University Press, 1999)
- Andrew Shonfield, *Modern Capitalism: The Changing Balance of Public and Private Power* (Oxford: Oxford University Press, 1965)

CHAPTER 4: WHO IS AGAINST EUROPE?

- Cécile Leconte, *Understanding Euroscepticism* (Basingstoke: Palgrave Macmillan, 2010)
- Peter Mair, *Ruling the Void: The Hollowing-Out of Western Democracy* (London: Verso, 2013)

- Hugo Young, *This Blessed Plot: Britain and Europe from Churchill to Blair* (London: Macmillan, 1998)

CHAPTER 5: WILL THE EU KEEP ON EXPANDING?

- Uwe W. Kitzinger, *Diplomacy and Persuasion: How Britain Joined the Common Market* (London: Thames and Hudson, 1973)
- Ivan Krastev, 'The Strange Death of the Liberal Consensus', *Journal of Democracy*, 18(4), October 2007, pp. 56–63
- Brendan Simms and Timothy Less, 'A crisis without end: The disintegration of the European project', *New Statesman*, 9 November 2015
- Jan Zielonka, *Europe as Empire: The Nature of the Enlarged European Union* (Oxford: Oxford University Press, 2006)

CHAPTER 6: COULD THE EU BECOME A SUPERPOWER?

- Christopher J. Bickerton, *European Union Foreign Policy: From Effectiveness to Functionality* (Basingstoke: Palgrave Macmillan, 2015)
- Robert Cooper, *The Breaking of Nations: Order and Chaos in the Twenty-First Century* (London: Atlantic, 2007)
- James Sheehan, *Where Have All the Soldiers Gone? The Transformation of Modern Europe* (Boston: Houghton Mifflin, 2008)

CONCLUSION: THE EU VERSUS DEMOCRACY

- Jürgen Habermas, *The Lure of Technocracy* (Cambridge: Polity, 2015)
- Ivan Krastev, 'A Fraying Union', *Journal of Democracy*, 23(4), 2012, pp. 23–30
- Claus Offe, *Europe Entrapped* (Cambridge: Polity, 2015)
- Wolfgang Streeck, *Buying Time: The Delayed Crisis of Democratic Capitalism* (London: Verso, 2014)
- Jan Zielonka, *Is the EU Doomed?* (Cambridge: Polity, 2014)

Index

Economics:
The User's Guide
Ha-Joon Chang

What is economics?

What can – and can't – it explain about the world?

Why does it matter?

Ha-Joon Chang teaches economics at Cambridge University and writes a column for the *Guardian*. The *Observer* called his book *23 Things They Don't Tell You About Capitalism*, which was a no.1 best-seller, 'a witty and timely debunking of some of the biggest myths surrounding the global economy'. He won the Wassily Leontief Prize for advancing the frontiers of economic thought and is a vocal critic of the failures of our current economic system.

A PELICAN
INTRODUCTION

Human Evolution
Robin Dunbar

What makes us human?

How did we develop language, thought and culture?

Why did we survive, and other human species fail?

Robin Dunbar is an evolutionary anthropologist and Director of the Institute of Cognitive and Evolutionary Anthropology at Oxford University. His acclaimed books include *How Many Friends Does One Person Need?* and *Grooming, Gossip and the Evolution of Language*, described by Malcolm Gladwell as 'a marvellous work of popular science'.

A PELICAN
INTRODUCTION

Revolutionary Russia, 1891–1991
Orlando Figes

What caused the Russian Revolution?

Did it succeed or fail?

Do we still live with its consequences?

Orlando Figes teaches history at Birkbeck, University of London and is the author of many acclaimed books on Russian history, including *A People's Tragedy*, which *The Times Literary Supplement* named as one of the '100 most influential books since the war', *Natasha's Dance*, *The Whisperers*, *Crimea* and *Just Send Me Word*. The *Financial Times* called him 'the greatest storyteller of modern Russian historians'.

A PELICAN
INTRODUCTION

The
Domesticated
Brain
Bruce Hood

Why do we care what others think?

What keeps us bound together?

How does the brain shape our behaviour?

Bruce Hood is an award-winning psychologist who has taught and researched at Cambridge and Harvard universities and is currently Director of the Cognitive Development Centre at the University of Bristol. He delivered the Royal Institution's Christmas Lectures in 2011 and is the author of *The Self Illusion* and *Supersense*, described by *New Scientist* as 'important, crystal clear and utterly engaging'.

A PELICAN
INTRODUCTION

Greek and
Roman
Political Ideas
Melissa Lane

**Where do
our ideas
about politics
come from?**

**What can we
learn from
the Greeks
and Romans?**

**How should
we exercise
power?**

Melissa Lane teaches politics
at Princeton University, and
previously taught for fifteen
years at Cambridge University,
where she also studied as a
Marshall and Truman scholar.
The historian Richard Tuck
called her book *Eco-Republic*
'a virtuoso performance by one
of our best scholars of ancient
philosophy'.

A PELICAN
INTRODUCTION

Classical
Literature
Richard Jenkyns

**What makes
Greek and Roman
literature great?**

**How has
classical literature
influenced
Western culture?**

**What did Greek
and Roman
authors learn
from each other?**

Richard Jenkyns is emeritus
Professor of the Classical
Tradition and the Public
Orator at the University of
Oxford. His books include
Virgil's Experience and *The
Victorians and Ancient Greece*,
acclaimed as 'masterly' by
History Today.

A PELICAN
INTRODUCTION

Who Governs Britain?
Anthony King

Where does power lie in Britain today?

Why has British politics changed so dramatically in recent decades?

Is our system of government still fit for purpose?

Anthony King is Millennium Professor of British Government at the University of Essex. A Canadian by birth, he broadcasts frequently on politics and government and is the author of many books on American as well as British politics. He is co-author of the bestselling *The Blunders of Our Governments*, which David Dimbleby described as 'enthralling' and Andrew Marr called 'an astonishing achievement'.

A PELICAN
INTRODUCTION

How to See the World
Nicholas Mirzoeff

**What is
visual culture?**

**How should we
explore the huge
quantity of visual
images available
to us today?**

**How can visual
media help
us change
the world?**

Nicholas Mirzoeff is Professor
of Media, Culture and
Communication at New York
University. His book *Watching
Babylon*, about the Iraq war as
seen on TV and in film, was
described by art historian Terry
Smith as 'a tour de force by
perhaps the most inventive –
certainly the most wide-ranging
– practitioner of visual culture
analysis in the world today.'

A PELICAN
INTRODUCTION

The Meaning of Science
Tim Lewens

What is science?

Where are its limits?

Can it tell us everything that is worth knowing?

Tim Lewens is a Professor of Philosophy of Science at Cambridge University, and a fellow of Clare College. He has written for the *London Review of Books* and *The Times Literary Supplement*, and has won prizes for both his teaching and his publications.

A PELICAN
INTRODUCTION

Social Class in the 21ˢᵗ Century
Mike Savage

Why does social class matter more than ever in Britain today?

How has the meaning of class changed?

What does this mean for social mobility and inequality?

Mike Savage is Professor of Sociology at the London School of Economics where he is also co-Director of the International Inequalities Institute. He is recognized as a leading international authority on social class, with his recent books including *Identities and Social Change in Britain Since 1940*. He has written this book in collaboration with the team of sociological experts linked to the Great British Class Survey: Niall Cunningham, Fiona Devine, Sam Friedman, Daniel Laurison, Lisa McKenzie, Andrew Miles, Helene Snee and Paul Wakeling.

A PELICAN
INTRODUCTION